D1418018

EATING ST. LOUIS:
THE GATEWAY CITY'S UNIQUE FOOD CULTURE

By Patricia Corrigan

**Doisy College of Health Sciences
at Saint Louis University**

Saint Louis University
221 N. Grand Blvd.
St. Louis, MO 63103

Published in cooperation with
Reedy Press
PO Box 5131
St. Louis, MO 63139

Please visit our website at www.reedypress.com.

Library of Congress Control Number:
2008930544

ISBN: 978-1-933370-70-5

Production Credits
Acquisitions Editor: Josh Stevens
Senior Editor: Charlotte Royeen
Associate Editor: Stephanie Collins-Batson
Associate Editor: Mildred Mattfeldt-Beman
Associate Editor: Mark Miller
Associate Editor: Todd Parkhurst
Production Manager: Matt Heidenry
Development Manager: Steve Sievers
Community Liaison: Joan Kiburz
Cover and Interior Design: Bruce Burton

Printed in China
08 09 10 11 12   5 4 3 2 1

O'Connell's Pub. Courtesy of Jack Parker.

For all the dedicated people in the metropolitan St. Louis area
who keep the rest of us well fed and watered

CONTENTS

FOREWORD

It is clear that St. Louisans have always loved good food. *Eating St. Louis* offers a peek into not only the history of what we eat, but also, since food is so reflective of our popular culture, how it has helped define who we are. So much attention has been paid to food and dining in recent years that it almost seems as if "food culture" is a modern phenomenon. Perhaps because more people are dining out now than in the recent past, restaurants play a much larger role in our day-to-day lives, but clearly a passion and an energy has long existed surrounding the dining scene in St. Louis.

So often when we talk about food in St. Louis, the focus is solely on restaurants, but the food industry extends far beyond the dining experience. *Eating St. Louis* not only delves into the intriguing past, but it also discusses the vibrant present of the various facets of this industry. Patricia has broken this book into five chapters, and the first is dedicated to restaurants. From there, Patricia weaves a flavorful tale of St. Louis's food manufacturers, grocers, farmers and farmers' markets, and finally breweries, wineries, and bars.

When I first spoke with Patricia regarding this book, I was—to be totally frank—a little skeptical that the many, many facets of St. Louis food could be compiled and condensed into one book. I stand corrected. Now, it is impossible to be comprehensive, but Patricia has offered a broad look at the people and products that define dining in St. Louis—from the history of Panera to Bill Keaggy's quirky grocery list collections; from the farmers that grow the produce at our fabulous farmers' markets to the characters that ran—and continue to run—the front of the house in our city's landmark restaurants; and from the long and significant history of beer production to the vineyards that surround the city. She has touched on what makes living and dining in St. Louis so unique and so flavorful.

As the editor of a culinary magazine, it is my job to keep current with what's new, what's fresh on the St. Louis scene. What people are craving today will not be what they want to cook tomorrow, and that's why working in the food industry is so dynamic. Restaurants open. Restaurants close. Chefs move from one kitchen to another. New wineries debut and each year put forth a new vintage. Markets shift their stock to accommodate our evolving tastes. There's always some new flavor, some new ingredient, or cooking method right around the corner.

Reading this book, however, reminded me to slow down a bit and look to our foodie past for inspiration as well. As we move further into this new century, we're learning more about how vital good food is to our overall health and well-being. We're also remembering how important it is to enjoy dining with others. While tastes change constantly, it seems that much of what was old is new again. And through it all, our city's food industry leaders' commitment to excellence hasn't wavered.

Catherine A. Neville
Editor in chief and co-founder, *Sauce Magazine*

PREFACE

Hail to food—food served in restaurants, food produced here and sold everywhere, food lining grocery aisles, fresh-picked food, and also to beverages served with all that food!

This book is a lavish buffet that offers something for everyone, a book to feed your curiosity, pique your interest in learning more, and make you proud to have a seat at the metropolitan area's table.

Stories about food and the people who produce, harvest, cook, and serve food fill these pages, some from days gone by, some from just a few months ago. Here, you will read stories about

- Josh Allen, who opened his wholesale business at the age of twenty-three
- Sinetsidk Berhanu, a grandmother from Ethiopia who advocates eating black lentils
- Gunnar Brown, master of a farmers' market who indulges in too many snow peas
- Jack Carl, a veteran of the Pastrami War of 1961 in Gaslight Square
- Lucian Dressel, who is breeding a new kind of wine grape for the Midwest
- Maddie Earnest, a grocer whose priority is to help support local food producers at her store
- Tony Faust, who sold five different kinds of oysters prepared twelve different ways at his restaurant here in 1899
- Ramon Gallardo, who boldly opened a Mexican restaurant devoid of sombreros
- Jake Hafner, who named his wine bar and shop after the year Prohibition was repealed
- Marge and Ed Imo, who started with a modest dream, a great idea, and some used pizza pans
- Mike Johnson, who opts to own several casual neighborhood places rather than one upscale restaurant
- Adolph Moll, who lured customers into his grocery in 1885 with a 2,300-pound wheel of cheese
- Lorenza Passeti, a third-generation *salumieri* who sells salami all over the world
- Michael Switzer, who has resurrected his grandfather's licorice business
- Bryan Truemper, a farmer who provides heirloom turkeys for Thanksgiving tables

These stories and more fill every page. Some of the stories will be new to you. Some, such as those about pork steaks and provel cheese, you may already know. Other all-too-familiar tales are purposely not told here, including stories about toasted ravioli (try them fresh-made at Trattoria Marcella or the Lombardo family restaurants), gooey butter cake (make your own at home), and St. Paul sandwiches (can I get that on whole wheat?).

One story you may not know is this: Tucked away on a university campus is a small café that serves as a microcosm for many of the themes expressed in this book. Chefs at Fresh Gatherings Café who serve as instructors at Saint Louis University's Doisy College of Health Sciences develop menus from produce and livestock raised within 150 miles of the campus.

Open to the public, the café is part of the Nutrition and Dietetics Department, which in 2001 introduced an innovative program that prepares dietetics students to become chefs as they work toward their registered dietetics and culinary arts credentials. Fresh Gatherings opened in 2004, when a food service company vacated the space that now houses the cafe.

"We were not interested in running a restaurant," says Mildred Mattfeldt-Beman, chairwoman of the Department of Nutrition and Dietetics. "When we introduced the culinary program, we wanted a culinary kitchen where students could get hands-on experience. We wanted a place run more like a café than a cafeteria, a place with an emphasis on a local sustainable food system that also would touch on social justice issues, environmental issues, and good nutrition."

For help in getting started, Mattfeldt-Beman approached Eddie Neill, a graduate of Saint Louis University who had co-owned and cooked at T.P. Neill's, Café Provencal, Chez Leon, Jazz at the Bistro, and Malmaison. (Today, Neill has The Dubliner, a European gastropub downtown.)

"I signed up to help at Fresh Gatherings for one year, and I stayed for two," says Neill. "I handled purchasing and much of the cooking, and I worked with undergraduate and graduate students." Todd Parkhurst, a former executive pastry chef who

Chef Mark Miller instructs students. Saint Louis University Department of Nutrition and Dietetics is the only academic department in the country to operate a restaurant that combines education, dietetics, and sustainable food systems. Courtesy of James Visser on behalf of Saint Louis University.

the best-selling food item was a grilled cheese sandwich. As the students' palates began to develop, stuffed portobellos, eggplant with chevre, and lamb stews took over as our more popular items. Now we don't sell one grilled cheese sandwich a week."

Michael Milster is the current chef, assisted by Parkhurst and Jamie Bommarito, a registered dietitian who also is a chef. Students, faculty, and members of the public who eat at Fresh Gatherings all are invested in the success of the café, and also in the philosophy of the café.

Fresh Gatherings also is now a key component of Mattfeldt-Beman's curriculum. In 2007, the café was remodeled to include a baking pastry lab with an open kitchen. When business is slow, students bake bread to sell at the Clayton Farmer's Market, with proceeds going to scholarships at the university. "Fresh Gatherings is something of a model nationally, and we have had schools visit from other parts of the country," says Mattfeldt-Beman. "I feel really good about what we are doing."

had worked in country clubs, restaurants, and hotels, came on as the baking instructor, and Stephanie Russell, formerly a chef at Whole Foods, also worked at Fresh Gatherings.

All three worked with the students to introduce as much texture and flavor to food as possible, using only a grill and an oven. "Some of the kids hated it," says Neill. "I was not using a fryer, and you would have thought I had run over their dog and killed their cat. But after a while, they got into it."

A deep fryer was left behind by the previous tenant, but Mattfeldt-Beman personally jerked it out and threw it away. "There was no way we were going to offer deep-fat fried anything," she says with a hearty laugh. "When Eddie first started,

Feeling good is what eating well is all about. Next best is reading about it. Go ahead—the delectable stories here are yours for the taking. Taste or inhale, nibble or gorge, stick with one plate or go back for thirds—or serve yourself sensible portions at reasonable intervals over time.

Patricia Corrigan

INTRODUCTION

It was my good fortune to spend many childhood summers in the St. Louis area (North Woodlawn in Kirkwood) with my aunt, uncle, and cousins, the Reichardts. My uncle worked for a major meat manufacturer in the region.

I grew up convinced of the following:

- Everyone eats pork steaks in the summer
- Braunschweiger is a typical American lunchmeat
- Sauerkraut is a condiment
- Horseradish is a condiment
- ReadyWhip goes with everything
- Families eat at a dinner table, with no TV!
- Ice cream, especially homemade and chocolate, is a staple of any diet
- Schnapps is a weekend drink
- Pot roast is always German-style sweet and sour
- Homemade jam is a part of everyday life, and:
- Pie is a normal part of every meal

Having spent considerable time outside of the St. Louis area, I have slowly come to realize that what had seemed usual and customary to me in everyday dining is, in fact, uniquely a part of St. Louis cuisine. Thus, I have been afforded a "big picture" view of St. Louis's unique dining delights, and these culinary habits became part of my family's tradition.

Related to this knowledge of the unique dining idiosyncrasies of the St. Louis region, I had other childhood misconceptions. While growing up in New Jersey, I thought that gardening with composted foodstuffs, natural habitat plants, and manure while using resources in a sustainable, locally grown manner was how all people gardened or farmed. In college, I finally realized, in retrospect, that my parents were somewhat eccentric—organic gardeners years before the term or practice was culturally popular. Let me assure you that not many high school students in New Jersey got to haul chicken manure as I did! Nor did many read the monthly magazine *Organic Gardener*.

Thus, not only did I think St. Louis dining habits were universal, I also believed organic gardening (and the tasty produce thereof) was normal.

Many years have passed since my life was enveloped by organic gardening in New Jersey and summertime dining in Kirkwood. Yet, these values remain. When I had the good fortune to become Dean of the Doisy College of Health Sciences of Saint Louis University, it was exciting to learn more about nutrition, dietetics, and culinary arts. It was especially exciting to work with Dr. Mildred Mattfeldt-Beman, chairperson of the Department of Nutrition and Dietetics, to transition the college's cafeteria from an external food service provider to the student laboratory, Fresh Gatherings™.

Fresh Gatherings is more directly addressed in the Preface and on page 136 of this book. Suffice to say that it is an integral part of one of only two academic programs in the United States that offers nutrition, dietetics, and culinary combined! (The other being at Johnson and Wales University.) Fresh Gatherings also offers manifestation of social justice values and beliefs, including:

- All people should have access to sustainable, locally grown food at an affordable price
- All students (from kindergarten through university) should be exposed to healthy eating
- The future of the United States is related to our view of sustainable food systems, healthy eating, and disease prevention via how we eat, and
- All food should be gourmet!

Finally, having been an academic writer, I find it natural to bring these threads (Fresh Gatherings and its philosophy of sustainability and the cuisine of St. Louis) together. Community leader Joan Kiburz inspired the creation of this book through her commitment to young girls in the inner city and healthy eating. (Be on the lookout for our second collaboration, *Making It*.) Through Doisy College of Health Sciences Marketing Manager Stephanie Collins-Batson, we discovered local publishers Josh Stevens and Matt Heidenry of Reedy Press. We, along with Dr. Mildred Mattfeldt-Beman and our chefs, formed a perfect partnership and collaboration with author Patricia Corrigan to conceptualize, develop, and produce the ultimate coffee table book befitting the great city of St. Louis. And this is how *Eating St. Louis: The Gateway City's Unique Food Culture* came to be.

In celebration of the great food culture of Saint Louis University's Doisy College of Health Sciences specifically and the city of St. Louis generally, I offer a poem as an invitation to one and all to try "eating St. Louis." The poem was written by octogenarian Gus G. Sotiropoulos, D.D.S., M.S., professor of Graduate Orthodontics and clinic director of the Center for Advanced Dental Education (CADE) of Saint Louis University. Most days, Dr. Sotiropoulos dines at Fresh Gatherings. During one of our routine exchanges about food at Fresh Gatherings and the food of St. Louis, he extemporaneously recited the following poem that captures what all of us at the Doisy College of Health Sciences and all over St. Louis believe about eating St. Louis.

As we invite you for a visit
to come and try our place to eat,
We know our food is so exquisite,
That many visits you'll repeat.

For food that has a wholesome savor
with taste appeal and zest,
We know you'll find no better flavor
than ours—for it is the best!

In closing, I want to acknowledge two important people whose work allowed this book to develop. One is the well-known gourmet and president of Saint Louis University, Father Lawrence Biondi. The other is Dr. Joe Weixlmann, the provost of Saint Louis University.

Charlotte Brasic Royeen, Dean
Doisy College of Health Sciences of Saint Louis University

EATING ST. LOUIS

Chapter 1

LET'S GO OUT TO EAT: RESTAURANTS

W hat are you in the mood for? We have cuisines from A (Afghan, African, American, Asian) to V (Vegan, Vegetarian, Vietnamese). In between, you can find restaurants specializing in Bosnian, Brazilian, Cajun, Chinese, Continental, Creole, Cuban, Ethiopian, French, Greek, Honduran, Indian, Irish, Italian, Jamaican, Japanese, Korean, Kosher, Lebanese, Mediterranean, Mexican, Middle Eastern, Nepali, Pakistani, Peruvian, Persian, Russian, Scottish, Serbian, Soul, Southern, Spanish, Thai, and Turkish foods.

Inset: Harry Karandzieff founded Crown Candy Kitchen in 1913 with his best friend, Pete Jugaloff.

Above: The staff is ready for the lunch rush in this photo by John Frangoulis. Courtesy Crown Candy Kitchen.

Previous Page: The Parkmoor at Clayton Road and Big Bend Boulevard, circa 1935. Courtesy of Missouri History Museum, St. Louis.

The metropolitan area is home to barbecue joints, bistros, brew pubs, cafeterias, chili parlors, delis, diners, egg roll kitchens, hamburger palaces, noodle shops, pizza places, seafood restaurants, soul food eateries, soup and sandwich shops, steakhouses, sushi bars, and tea rooms. You may dine in, carry out, take delivery, or order catered meals for breakfast, brunch, lunch, a pre-theater nosh, dinner, a snack after the game, dessert, or a late-night bite.

Ahi? Baklava? Crepes? Dim Sum? We've got 'em all. Escargot? Falafel? Guacamole? Hash browns? Look no further. Injera? Jambalaya? Kibbeh? Lasagna? Yep. Moussaka? Nachos? Omelets? Pad Thai? You bet. Red beans and rice? Spinach pies? Tapas? Udon? Oh yeah. Vichyssoise? Welsh rarebit? Zabaglione? Absolutely!

SAUCE MAGAZINE:
A FILLING SOURCE FOR FOOD NEWS

Catherine Neville (left) and Allyson Mace. Courtesy of Sauce Magazine.

Catherine Neville, co-founder with Allyson Mace and the editor in chief of *Sauce Magazine* and saucemagazine. com, spends her days writing about food, reading about food, and thinking about food.

"I have always loved food, and I have always wanted to be in the magazine business," says Neville. When she was fourteen, Neville and her best friend, Heather Cordon (now Heather Cordon Wilson), produced, directed, and starred in *Cathi's Kitchen*, a cooking show that included commercials. The girls baked cakes in Neville's parents' kitchen in O'Fallon, Illinois, and her ten-year-old brother David taped the shows.

Before Mace served as director of operations for *Sauce*, she worked for fifteen years in the restaurant industry welcoming guests, managing, tending bar, and serving food. Her father, the late Eugene A. Mace, owned newspapers elsewhere in Missouri and was inducted into the Missouri Newspaper Hall of Fame in 2001. Mace's mother, Janet, still owns the *Ste. Genevieve Herald*.

"Think about it," says Neville. "Publishing and the restaurant business are two of the most volatile businesses around. Imagine running a restaurant magazine! What is the likelihood of our success?"

The question is moot.

In April 2008, the circulation of *Sauce Magazine* was 84,000 and growing with each month's issue. More than forty people contribute to *Sauce*, and Neville and

The first issue. Courtesy of Sauce Magazine.

Mace employee additional editors, designers, sales staff, and distribution staff. Neville also is on television and radio every week, talking about food and restaurants.

The web site came first, in 1999. "In 1998, Allyson was in the restaurant industry and I was an editor and web designer at Washington University," recalls Neville. "We talked about how there wasn't much on the Internet about local restaurants, and St. Louis has a lot of great places to eat. We decided to put together a web site."

That web site's popularity grew slowly, organically—mostly by word of mouth. In October 2001, Mace and Neville started a print edition of saucemagazine.com. The first issue was just sixteen pages long, with a two-color cover. A typical issue of Sauce today is sixty-eight pages, filled with feature articles, reviews, recipes, and interviews. The magazine also covers the local bar and music scene and the art world in St. Louis.

In April 2005, Neville and Mace launched TheDailySauce. com, a "bite" of information on dining or food sent to subscribers via email. Saucegifts.com was up and running in November 2005, and SauceClassifieds.com started in June 2007.

"We started the web site, the magazine—all of this—to celebrate what makes St. Louis a great place to live. We have a great independent restaurant scene here, with plenty of creative owners, chefs, bartenders, and other people in the industry," says Neville. "And here we are, almost ten years later—that's amazing!"

Neville continues: "What was true in 1999 is true now: People love food. We're lucky to be living in a time when people are interested in learning about food, a time when dining out is not just for special occasions, a time when people don't want to go to the same places over and over."

Neville smiles and adds, "Looking back, I feel like I'm where I should be, doing what I should be doing."

The Gateway City and environs has gourmet food, low food, fast food, and slow food. We have a vintage malt shop that opened in 1913—Crown Candy Kitchen, north of downtown. We have old favorites, tried-and-true restaurants, as well as a slew of contemporary hot spots. Among the latter is Niche, in Benton Park, where chef and owner Gerard Craft was hailed as one of 10 Best New Chefs by *Food & Wine Magazine* in April 2008. In 2007, Craft was named Chef of the Year by *Sauce Magazine* and Best Local Chef by the *Riverfront Times.*

Our local eateries pop up all the time on The Food Network. The Blue Owl, City Diner, Cunetto's, Fitz's, Iron Barley, Sweetie Pie's, and Top of the Riverfront all have been featured recently. That's not all: St. Louis takes credit for inventing the slinger, which consists of two burger patties, hash browns, and an egg, all covered with chili and served with toast. The dish was devised in the 1980s at the O.T. Hodge Chile Parlor, an establishment founded by a local barber in 1904.

About 4,800 restaurants currently operate in the metropolitan area, and about 60 percent of them are independently owned. "That's good—real good," says Pat Bergauer, executive vice president and eastern regional director of the Missouri Restaurant Association. She adds that about fifty new restaurants open here each year, most often more independents.

"This is a great time to live and eat in the St. Louis area," notes Bergauer. "In my opinion, there is no better person than someone who decides to get into the restaurant business. To do that, you have to like people and you have to enjoy watching customers enjoy themselves. Customers can always feel that warmth."

Missouri boasts close to 11,000 restaurants. Nationally, there are 935,000 eating establishments that employ 12.8 million people and bring in some $537 billion a year, according to the National Restaurant Association. Here are some more fun facts:

- On a typical day, 132 million individuals in the United States will eat out.

- The restaurant industry's share of the food dollar today is 47.9 percent, compared to 25 percent in 1955.

- Nationally, restaurant industry sales on a typical day are $1.5 billion.

- Four out of five customers say that going out to a restaurant is a better way to use their leisure time than cooking and cleaning up.

Restaurant owners here and elsewhere are well aware of the public's interest in locally produced products. The National Restaurant Association reports that 86 percent of fine-dining restaurants serve locally sourced food items.

THE MISSOURI RESTAURANT ASSOCIATION

Pat Bergauer

The Missouri Restaurant Association, with headquarters in Maryland Heights, is among the five largest restaurant associations in the nation. Ten affiliate chapters in the state represent a membership of over four thousand eating establishments.

Size matters—but so does longevity.

The restaurant trade association movement traces its roots to Missouri. In 1916, local restaurant operators founded the Kansas City Business Men's Association. In 1919, these same individuals gathered other restaurateurs from around the nation to form the National Restaurant Association. Originally, the organization was based in Kansas City until 1926, when the office was moved to Chicago.

In 1935, charters were granted to both the Missouri Restaurant Association and the St. Louis Restaurant Association. In 1958, several city associations chose to band together, and four years later, the Kansas City and St. Louis associations agreed to affiliate as chapters of the Missouri Restaurant Association.

Courtesy of Missouri Restaurant Association

OUR OLDEST, ALMOST OLDEST, AND MOST DECORATED RESTAURANTS

The oldest continuously operating restaurant in town is Beffa's, at 2700 Olive Street downtown. Records show that members of the Beffa family from Switzerland opened a restaurant downtown in 1898. Their descendants now own Beffa's.

You say you've never heard of it?

That's not surprising. No sign directs diners to Beffa's, and the eatery is not listed in the telephone book. If by chance you do find the restaurant and go inside, you will see plenty of local movers and shakers—but no menus.

Is this any way to run a restaurant?

Apparently so—it has worked well for 110 years!

Busch's Grove was established before Beffa's but has not stayed open from the start. In 1830, the Woodlawn Grove—a gathering place, general store, and post office—opened at what is now 9160 Clayton Road in Ladue.

In 1890, John Busch bought the Woodlawn Grove, and six years later, he opened Busch's Grove, serving family recipes from Switzerland. St. Louisans traveled from the city to the restaurant in horse-drawn carriages. After a long run, Busch's Grove closed in 2003. Lester Miller renovated the property and reopened the restaurant in 2005. He put it up for sale in May 2008.

Tony's, at 410 Market Street, is "the most-decorated restaurant in Missouri," says Vincent J. Bommarito, who owns and operates the restaurant with his sons. Famous for fine dining, Tony's routinely is acclaimed by national, regional, and local reviewers. Among the many honors presented to Tony's is the coveted AAA five-diamond award. Only thirty-four restaurants in North America have received it, and Tony's is the only restaurant in Missouri to be so honored.

The Bommarito family upholds a long tradition of fine dining at Tony's, shown above. Courtesy of Vincent J. Bommarito.

As a young man, Bommarito had worked just one summer as a bus boy at his father's restaurant, a popular spaghetti house downtown also known as Tony's, before his father died in 1949. "My mother said I should take over the restaurant," says Bommarito. "She said if I couldn't make a go of it, I could go back to school."

Bommarito more than made a go of it. Today, he holds the title of chairman at Tony's. His sons all have followed their father into the business. Vincent P. Bommarito is president at Tony's, Anthony L. Bommarito is vice president, and James D. Bommarito is secretary-treasurer.

The management philosophy at Tony's is simple. "We are service-oriented. Every night, no matter what, at 5:30 everything else stops and we focus exclusively on the guests," says Bommarito. "We used to say we wanted to meet expectations. Now we say we want to exceed expectations."

Ask Bommarito about the history of restaurants in St. Louis, and he tells great tales of crowds disembarking from the *Admiral* at 11 p.m. on summer nights and stopping at Tony's for big bowls of spaghetti and loaves of Italian bread. "Today, no one's cardiologist will permit that," says Bommarito, laughing. "Those were the days."

He speaks highly of other restaurant owners of the time, as well. "Mrs. Kemoll was a pioneer, always bringing back new dishes from Italy. Mrs. Baronni ran Al's, and she was the first to do a limited menu," Bommarito recalls. "Mrs. Yoast had the Hitching Post, where you could get a biscuit casserole and fresh apple butter. And Miss Hulling's was the best restaurant in the country for breakfast—she had pan-fried sausage with country gravy, homemade biscuits or cornbread, and fresh juice."

Florence Hulling started working as a waitress at Child's, on Seventh Street near Olive, when she was thirteen years old. That's where she met her husband, Stephen Apted. In 1934, the two opened their first cafeteria at Eighth and Olive. Customers quickly became enamored with the home-style food served by Miss Florence, Miss Mary, and Miss Beulah. By 1967, Miss Florence and her son, Steve Apted, owned six restaurants in town, including Cheshire. Miss Hulling's restaurants are long gone, but Straub's Market sells the ever-popular split-layer cakes.

Another popular restaurateur, in business from 1933 through 1968, was Mina Evans, the longtime owner of the Golden Fried Chicken Loaf. "Mom would fry a whole cut-up chicken and place all the pieces on a four-and-a-half-inch-wide loaf of buttered, toasted French bread," says Mina Overton, Evans'

Mina Evans (second from right) accepts one of many awards for her restaurant. Courtesy of Mina Overton.

The rich and famous—and many others as well—dined at the Planters House Hotel, at one time the largest hotel in the country. Courtesy of the Library of Congress.

daughter. "That was a golden fried chicken loaf, and the loaves were served on oval platters."

Another specialty of the house at 5865 Delmar was chicken dumpling soup, made with spaetzle noodles. Evans also was known for her pies. "People loved Mom's pies—apple, strawberry, and chocolate especially," says Overton. "She sold them by the piece in the restaurant, but she also sold them whole. Some days, she sold three hundred pies."

Originally, the Golden Fried Chicken Loaf was a small place, but it grew swiftly. "In its heyday, there were forty employees and a big private dining room for parties," recalls Overton. "At one point, my mother raised her own chickens and also butchered her own cattle. Eventually, my father, Omar Evans, took over the ranches and managed the cattle."

Overton and her brother, Omar Evans, worked at the Golden Fried Chicken Loaf on weekends and in the summer when they were home from college, but Overton's work history at the restaurant goes back even further. "When I was a little kid, I'd go in and swat flies in the kitchen. I'd get a penny for every fly."

At one time, the best restaurants in St. Louis were in hotels, including the Statler, the Mayfair, the Jefferson, and the George Washington. When the twenty-four-story Lennox Hotel opened in 1929, it was the largest hotel in town.

The Planters House Hotel, originally at Chestnut and Pine, was built in 1841 to accommodate three hundred guests, which made it one of the largest hotels in the country. A year later, Charles Dickens stayed at the hotel. (His comment about the bar there is in Chapter 5.) Just over one hundred years later, in 1945, a steak at the Planters House Hotel cost forty-five cents, which was considered outrageous at the time.

George S. Beers built his Hotel Beers in 1868 at Twenty-ninth and Olive, and twenty years later he published a booklet touting his place as "The Most Complete Restaurant and Catering Establishment in the West." The booklet includes his catering menu, an etiquette guide for social functions, and recipes, including one for chicken croquettes that begins, "Select one good hen."

FAUST'S: OUR FIRST FAMOUS RESTAURANT

Today, the Adams Mark Hotel downtown houses a restaurant called Faust's, an historic name in St. Louis. Tony Faust opened his first restaurant at Broadway and Elm Streets next to the Southern Hotel, which was built in 1866. A fire in 1877 took the hotel and the restaurant, too. After a trip to Europe, Faust returned to St. Louis in 1878 and built a new place with a lighting system and lamps that he had seen at the Paris Exposition.

Newspaper accounts of the day reported that the lights—the first in St. Louis—were "a source of amusement and wonder," and that people (those who were not afraid of the lights) "stood for hours and watched them." According to an article in the *Globe-Democrat* on June 26, 1927, Faust's was one of the best advertisements St. Louis ever had "in the days when men were regular both with their meals and with their drinking."

The restaurant was known nationally for its seafood, roasts, stews, and beer. The menu for an end-of-the-year banquet held on December 29, 1896, consisted of consommé royal, stuffed olives with celery, filet of Spanish mackerel, iced cucumbers, saddle of venison, imported asparagus, pressed wood duck, chicory and watercress salad, a sweet omelet, cheese, and coffee. Oh, there was one more course. In between the imported asparagus and the pressed wood duck, diners were served "Egyptianne Cigarettes."

In 1889, Faust built a two-story brick restaurant that accommodated one thousand people. The oaken bar was on the street level, with half a dozen bartenders serving drinks to over one hundred men. Upstairs, Faust's had an "air of sober elegance," and a Millionaire's Table. Adolphus Busch, who made a pale lager named for his friend, sat there, as did William Lemp, another successful brewery owner. They dined on quail served atop sauerkraut, and on oysters, raw or fried, that cost twenty-five cents for half a dozen.

Left: The Tyrolean Alps Restaurant at the 1904 World's Fair charged $1.25 for filet mignon. Courtesy of Missouri History Museum, St. Louis.

Right: Faust's, shown here in circa 1885, put St. Louis on the map as a city known for good food. Courtesy of Missouri History Museum, St. Louis.

Oysters, brought in from the East Coast packed in ice, were a specialty of the house at Faust's. A menu dated September 6, 1899, offers five different kinds ("Blue Pointe, Rockaway, Shrewsbury, Saddle Rock, and East River") prepared twelve different ways ("raw, stew, pan roast, fancy roast, roast in the shell, broiled, Boston stew, Baltimore dry stew, cream stew, fried, scalloped, or in an oyster loaf").

At the 1904 World's Fair, Tony Faust and August Luchow of New York City opened the Tyrolean Alps Restaurant, which seated twenty-five-hundred customers. At the time, caviar or soft-shelled crabs cost seventy-five cents and a filet mignon sold for $1.25. Two years later, Faust died. His obituary ran in the local papers and also in the *New York Times*. He is buried in Bellefontaine Cemetery.

Throughout World War I, Prohibition, and the Depression, most St. Louisans lived modestly, eating and entertaining at home much of the time, even on special occasions. In the 1940s, interest in dining out returned. People headed out for hearty food at cafeterias, in hotel coffee shops, and in neighborhood restaurants.

GONE BUT NOT FORGOTTEN: MEDART'S, DRIVE-INS, AND DEPARTMENT STORE DINING ROOMS

In the late 1930s, Bill Medart opened a luncheonette in a log cabin, part of which still stands today at Clayton Road and Skinker where the Cheshire Restaurant once was (and the Cheshire Inn still is). Medart's was known for spaghetti served in a skillet, but the true specialty of the house was hamburgers, served with a mayonnaise-based sauce and wrapped in a folded napkin.

"There was something about those hamburgers," says Harold D. Russell. "They cost thirty-five cents. That was kind of high, but for a good one you'd pay it—and Medart's hamburgers were really good."

Russell, a former prizefighter and recent recipient of the Gold Medal Award from the Society of American Magicians, is eighty-six years old. In 1952, he worked several nights a week as a doorman and valet for the Rose and Crown, the Medart family's upscale restaurant at the same location. "You got to know people, and they got to know you," Russell recalls. "I got tips—usually twenty-five cents, but sometimes a dollar. On a big night, I'd make forty dollars."

Medart's is gone today, but John Ruprecht serves their famous burgers at his Town Hall Restaurant at 665 South Skinker. "Our chef developed it," says Ruprecht, whose restaurant has been at its current location since 1971. "We serve it with the special sauce, lettuce, pickles, and onion, on a bun, and it's wrapped in a napkin."

With a few exceptions, drive-in hamburger joints (not to be confused with drive-through hamburger joints) are a thing of the past. Even before drive-ins, there were diners. In the 1920s, a diner was a single-unit, prefabricated structure, assembled and then delivered to a neighborhood corner. Inside, customers sat on stools at long counters and in booths that lined a wall of windows.

Harold D. Russell recalls making those hamburgers from Medart's disappear—but today, he is renowned as a close-up magician. His philosophy of life is simple: Expect Magic.

"HACK" ULRICH: CHASING A LEGEND

One night in 1952 when Frank Sinatra failed to show up for a gig at the Chase Hotel, someone had to tell the standing-room-only crowd that Sinatra would not be appearing. That unpleasant task fell to Henry "Hack" G. Ulrich, Jr., who worked as a manager at the Chase Club until it closed in 1961, and then spent thirty-five years as the maitre d' at the hotel's Tenderloin Room.

As recounted by Ulrich in 1998, Sinatra missed the gig here because he was in New York "pleading with Ava Gardner to come back to him." Sinatra did show up to sing the rest of the week, but Ulrich told a *Post-Dispatch* reporter that Ol' Blue Eyes was so upset that he did just five or six numbers at each show.

Ulrich had a different work record. "Dad did not miss a day of work in fifty years," recalls Richard Ulrich, a St. Louis–based lawyer. "He loved his work, and he was just phenomenal—the most generous, kindest man that ever lived. Every one of his employees would have run through walls for him."

After graduating from high school, Hack worked as a bus boy at a country club for a few months and then took the job at the Chase. "This was in the heyday of the Chase Hotel, a period that ran from the late 1940s through the early 1960s," says Ulrich.

In their book *Dining In—St. Louis*, J.A. Baer and Cecile K. Lowenhaupt describe the Tenderloin Room in 1979: "To step into the Tenderloin Room is to take a step back in time into the opulent Victorian era of ornately carved mahogany, massive brass chandeliers, gilt and marble mantelpieces. Maitre d' Hack Ulrich presides. He has greeted presidents and kings, first ladies and queens, with grace and hospitality. The same welcome awaits you."

Ulrich recalls that his father met seven or eight presidents but was as friendly toward his co-workers as any high-ranking government officials or movie stars. "He had a magnetic charisma and could talk to anyone," he says. "He liked people, and he was content with what he had."

"Hack" Ulrich retired in 1992 and died in 2002.

Hack Ulrich (left) converses with a waiter. Courtesy of Richard Ulrich

The Chase•Park Plaza

Diners defined themselves by their simple menu, typically burgers and breakfast foods prepared on a griddle by spatula-wielding short-order cooks, usually male. Chili and soups, too, were always available at diners. Blame the drive-in hamburger stands and the fast-food industry for pushing diners from public consciousness. By the mid-1960s, suddenly no one had time to linger over a piece of pie and a cup of coffee at the neighborhood diner.

In the late 1970s, when diners enjoyed a momentary comeback, the Webster Grill opened in Webster Groves as a new-age diner complete with stools at the counter, serving stir-frys and falafel in addition to more typical diner fare. The Parkmoor, which opened in 1930 at Clayton Road and Big Bend Boulevard as a drive-in, evolved into a diner with seven locations. Keeping pace with the times, the Parkmoor re-invented itself yet again, offering an expanded menu in an effort to be all things to all people. That worked well for a while, but the last Parkmoor closed in 1999.

Diners do play a part in today's restaurant scene. The Courtesy Diner, an institution at 3153 South Kingshighway for over forty years, now has a second location at 1121 Hampton Avenue. Richard Connelly operates the Goody Goody Diner, at 5900 Natural Bridge Avenue. The Goody Goody opened in 1931 as a root beer stand, but by 1948 it had evolved into a drive-in. Over time, the Goody Goody dropped the carhops and curb service and began operating as a diner. Herb and Viola Connelly bought the restaurant in 1954, and today, the smoke-free Goody Goody still packs in the people.

Like the Goody Goody, Carl's Drive-In, at 9033 Manchester, is firmly rooted in a neighborhood. In the 1930s, what is now Carl's was a gas station where you also could fill up on a hot dog and a glass of root beer. Carl Meyer bought the place in 1959. He operated Carl's as a drive-in for a short time, but by 1962, the place had evolved into a diner. Twenty-five years later, Frank Cunetto took over Carl's, and he's there almost every day, cooking hamburgers and onion rings and serving homemade root beer.

Department stores moved more than merchandise after the turn of the century. A menu dated 1915 from the Famous-Barr Dairy Lunch Room listed corned beef sandwiches for ten cents, Norwegian sardines with potato salad for twenty-five cents, and stewed prunes for five cents. The department store lunch counters are now a part of St. Louis's collective memory. Some of those memories are pleasant; some are not.

In 1944, an interracial group of women, part of the Citizens' Civil Rights Committee, began holding sit-ins at department store lunch counters downtown. Three years later, the local branch of the Congress of Racial Equality (CORE) organized a non-violent campaign that included negotiations and sit-ins at department store lunch counters, restaurants, movie theaters, and hotels. These actions and those that followed led to a city-wide ban in 1961 on discrimination in public accommodations.

In the 1950s, many a local grill offered copy-cat blue-plate specials that included a choice of fresh-roasted turkey, roast beef, ham, and stews, served with mashed potatoes and gravy. The food industry "grew like crazy from 1960 on," recalls Stanley Allen, former owner of Allen Foods, which distributed food to restaurants, hotels, long-term care facilities, and educational institutions in St. Louis, Kansas City, and Southern Illinois. "More people were eating out, disposable income changed when more women went to work—and we were there, along with a lot of competition, supplying restaurants." Allen's biggest seller was a cocktail mix that served as the base for many a margarita made all over the country.

Remember when New York–style cheesecake showed up on almost every menu in town? Allen gets credit for that, too. "We started making cheesecake in 1971, and it caught on quickly. First, we sold plain, and then we added turtle and strawberry swirl," he says. "That cheesecake was a terrific product. Everything in it was natural."

Everything in the outrageous desserts at Cyrano's was loaded with calories, but back then, nobody cared. People stood in line to be admitted to the restaurant's basement location on Clayton Road at DeMun Avenue, where they ordered exotic flaming desserts and ice cream sundaes topped with mounds of whipped cream. The current incarnation of Cyrano's is in Webster Groves—and yes, you can still order Cherries Jubilee.

Courtesy of Goody Goody Diner

JOE AND ANN LEMONS POLLACK: PROFESSIONAL DINERS

Courtesy of Rudie Erschen

On Christmas Eve about a decade ago, Ann Lemons Pollack and Joe Pollack were having dinner at a curry house in Singapore. They were sharing a bowl of fish head curry. "After the waiter divided up the sweet, succulent cheeks, all that remained was the eye," recalls Ann. "Joe got it."

Adventurous eating—that's what it takes to earn the iconic status that Joe and Ann have achieved in this town. Their books include *The Great St. Louis Eats Book, Beyond Toasted Ravioli,* and *Beyond Gooey Butter Cake,* and their online reviews appear at www. stlouiseats.typepad.com.

Joe, who was inducted into the St. Louis Media Hall of Fame in 2008, has been a writer for more than a half century and also has reported for radio and television. He started in public relations with the National Football League, and worked for the *Post-Dispatch* for twenty-three years, where he was a theater critic, movie critic, wine writer, and restaurant critic. Currently, Joe is the theater and film critic for KWMU-FM Radio. Before he joined the *Post-Dispatch* staff in the 1960s, he sold freelance stories to the paper about restaurants.

"Over the years you develop judgment about what preparations are right and what are not as they should be. One thing that has made me semi-successful is that I like most everything," says Joe. "I've always been a big meat eater, and a seafood lover. My parents took me to restaurants in New York when I was growing up. I remember eating Japanese food—tempura, sukiyaki—before World War II, at restaurants on Fifty-Sixth Street."

Ann, who grew up in Desloge, Missouri, claims she was a picky eater as a child. "I was a fearful eater. I lived in horror of eating something that I would not like," she says. "I remember my father gently persuading me to try limeade at a soda fountain at Walgreen's in Hot Springs, Arkansas."

Ann continues: "At nineteen, I forced myself to branch out. I discovered I could tolerate things I didn't like by taking a bite of rice or bread and then a bite of what I didn't like. Finally, I started eating like a grownup." As a grownup, Ann has written about cooking, eating, shopping, travel, and dining out for *St. Louis Magazine,* the *Post-Dispatch,* and other regional publications.

"I'm glad I don't live in New York and go traveling and think, 'This food is not as good as where I live'—because then there is nothing to explore," says Ann. "That said, for its size, St. Louis is very lucky in terms of the quality of food here."

Joe adds, "I have learned not to argue with people about pizza and barbecue, because so many people have strong opinions on those." What's his favorite cuisine? He laughs. "Whatever I had last." About that fish eye in Singapore—Joe chose not to eat it. He grins and says, "It disappeared under a lettuce leaf."

FRESH RESPECT

In 1970, Richard Perry opened the Jefferson Avenue Boarding House. (Have you figured out where it was located? Good.) Perry, brought up on a farm, is a pioneer in American cookery, a man who promoted using fresh regional products before Alice Waters thought to try that. Over the years, Perry has collected the following honors:

- First Fifty Who's Who in American Cooking,
  Cook's magazine

- Top One Hundred Restaurants in America,
  Playboy magazine

- One of Fifty Best New American Restaurants,
  Esquire magazine

- *Travel/Holiday Magazine* Award

- *Mobil Guide* Four-Star Award

- One of Six Most Romantic Dining Spots,
  USA Today

- Featured on NBC *Today Show*

"Yeah, that and a nickel . . ." says Perry with a hearty laugh. "Awards don't translate into any big deal, though it's nice to be noticed. Before I started cooking, I worked for McGraw-Hill, and when I traveled, people took me to restaurants, usually steakhouses or pseudo-continental places. I remember thinking how nice it would be to open a restaurant and serve home-cooked food. Eventually, that's what I did."

To date, Perry has owned or operated nine restaurants, all but three of them in the metropolitan area. His most recent venture, with co-owner James Russell, was the Farmer's Inn and Prairie Kitchen in Millstadt. Today, Perry operates his Eat Plan program, which delivers meals to clients too busy to cook. "My philosophy about food has not changed," says Perry. "Even today, I think following a fad or a trend from somewhere else just doesn't have the ring of truth to it."

Like Perry, Eddie Neill is bemused by the recent buzz about building menus around locally grown products. Neill, who has been involved with eight restaurants (most recently The Dubliner, downtown), has always followed that philosophy. Along with Andy Ayers at Riddle's Penultimate in the University City Loop and other local chefs interested in sustainable food, Neill founded a chef's collaborative that resulted in the genesis of the Clayton Farmer's Market. (For more information on that market and others, see Chapter 4.)

"My father and grandfather were farmers, and what should have been the norm by now is suddenly a trend," says Neill. "Some people who are following the trend are not doing it out of proper respect for the food. The point is, and always has been, what better food is there than something fresh?"

Richard Perry

Eddie Neill. Courtesy of Katherine Bish.

FAMILY CONNECTIONS

You already know that about 60 percent of local restaurants here are independently owned and operated. Who are some of the families that feed us? A number of restaurant owners got their start working at Tony's. Here is a partial list:

- Benedetto Buzzetta (Benedetto's)
- William Cramer, Jr. (Cramer's)
- Andrino di Santos (Andrino's)
- Agostino Gabriele (Agostino's Colosseum Restaurant)
- Giovanni Gabriele (Giovanni's on the Hill)
- Dominic Galati (Dominic's on the Hill and Dominic's Trattoria)
- Charlie Gitto, Jr. (Charlie Gitto's on the Hill)
- Paul Manno (Paul Manno's Café)
- John Mineo (John Mineo's Italian Restaurant)
- Bill Politis (Majestic Restaurant)
- John Saputo (John Saputo's)

J. Kim Tucci also is a graduate of Vincent J. Bommarito University. Now co-owner with Joe Fresta of The Pasta House Co., Tucci worked at Tony's as a parking lot attendant, doorman, maitre d', assistant waiter, waiter, and assistant manager. "The

reason I learned so much when I worked at Tony's was that I never thought I'd open a restaurant," says Tucci. "Mainly I was Vince's assistant, so I learned everything firsthand."

Another fellow with plenty of firsthand knowledge is Paul A. Manno, thirty-four, owner of the restaurant that bears his name in Chesterfield. "My dad, Paul Manno, came to St. Louis with his father, Paolo Manno, in 1956 because my grandfather had a brother and cousins living here. The idea was to work and send money back to Sicily so my dad's sisters could come here, too," Manno explains.

Those sisters—Rosa, Anna, Fina, Concetta, and Lia—did come to St. Louis, and they married Agostino Gabriele, John Mineo, Giovanni Gabriele, Franco Sanfilippo, and Benedetto Buzzetta, respectively. Manno's dad married Concetta di Natale.

Paul's father worked at Tony's fourteen years, from 1960 to 1974. "My dad was not in the restaurant business when he came here, and neither were my uncles, though Uncle Agostino had cooked in the Italian Merchant Marine," says Manno. "It must have been great for Vince Bommarito, having all these Italians fresh from the boat, ready to learn. Then, as opportunities arose, they all left Tony's and went on to open their own restaurants."

Top left: Bart Saracino, Sr. (holding plaque) was inducted into the Missouri Restaurant Association Hall of Fame in 2002. From left are Joe Weiman, Chris Saracino, Michael Saracino, Bart Saracino, Sr., Bart Saracino, Jr., and John Saracino. Courtesy of Missouri Restaurant Association.

Above: Paul A. Manno (left) learned the restaurant trade from his father, Paul, and his mother, Concetta. Courtesy Paul A. Manno.

Mr. and Mrs. Kemoll with their son-in-law, Frank J. Cusumano, Sr., in the Florentine Room at the old Kemoll's on North Grand. Courtesy of Ellen Cusumano.

After he left Tony's, Paul's dad went into business with his brother-in-law, John Mineo. He later opened Ciao in St. Charles.

In October 1995, the Mannos opened Paul Manno's Café in Chesterfield. "We had both places going at first, and it was tough," recalls Manno. "My mom would make tomato sauce in St. Charles and I'd go pick it up." In 1996, the family closed Ciao and their son took over as owner at Paul Manno's Café, where he cooks, serves, greets customers, cleans mirrors, and often straightens one of the many photos of Frank Sinatra.

"I show up, and I do what I know how to do," says Manno. "I'm in this business because I want to be. All those years, seeing my dad's personality, seeing how he is with people, and then going in the kitchen and seeing my mom's passion for cooking—that was huge. I'm putting all that together."

Other offspring from the extended family have also "put it all together." Frank and Carmelo Gabriele, sons of Giovanni Gabriele, own Il Bel Lago in Creve Coeur. Joe Sanfilippo owns J.F. Sanfilippo's downtown. John and Paul Gabriele are at Agostino's in Ellisville. John Mineo, Jr., is at John Mineo's Italian Restaurant in Town and Country, and Paul Mineo recently opened Paul Mineo's Trattoria at Westport.

Is Paul A. Manno intimidated by the legacy his father and his other relatives have established, or the high standards his cousins have set for their restaurants? "No," he says, smiling. "I'm just working hard to bring the best of the Italian food that I know to everyone in St. Louis." That works—in both the 2007 and 2008 guides to America's 1,000 Top Italian Restaurants, the Zagat Survey rated Paul Manno's Café the best Italian Restaurant in St. Louis.

Other local families have built a legacy in St. Louis in the restaurant business. Ellen Cusumano represents the fourth generation in her family to work in the business, and rumor has it that the fifth generation is already "chipping in." Cusumano works at Kemoll's, which started out in 1927 as a small confectionary selling sandwiches, candy, and Italian ices.

In the 1960s, Kemoll's on North Grand was a destination restaurant, featuring international dishes served on "Gourmet Nights." In 1990, fourth-generation family member Mark Cusumano moved Kemoll's to its current location in One Metropolitan Square downtown, where Sicilian specialties and authentic international dishes are on the menu.

Four generations have worked at Yacovelli's, which was founded in 1919 by John Yacovelli, who immigrated from San Salvatori, Italy. His son, Dewey Yacovelli, is said to have originated the idea of the salad bar. John Yacovelli's grandson, Jack, and his family now run the restaurant, which has been located in Florissant since 1977. The Missouri Restaurant Association named Jack and Jan Yacovelli as the 2007 Restaurateurs of the Year.

KEMOLL'S
Since 1927

Three generations of the Karagiannis family have made feeding St. Louisans their business. In 1956, Gus Karagiannis and his wife left Greece. Today, their children and grandchildren own and operate seven local restaurants:

- Pepperstone Steakhouse at 1287 Jungermann Road in St. Peters
- Spiro's North at 8406 Natural Bridge in Bel-Nor
- Spiro's Restaurant at 3122 Watson Road in St. Louis
- Spiro's West at 1054 North Woods Mill Road in Chesterfield
- Spiro's St. Charles at 2275 Bluestone Drive in St. Charles
- Surf & Sirloin at 13090 Manchester in Des Peres
- The Tenderloin Room in the Chase-Park Plaza Hotel in St. Louis

Mike Slay and Francis R. Slay converse near a photo of their father, Joseph Slay, on the wall at Slay's of Grantwood. Courtesy of Francis G. Slay.

"Growing up in the restaurant business, everybody who worked for my family was treated like family. When you got married, you went to the restaurant in your wedding clothes to say hello to everyone in the kitchen," recalls Slay. "Also, Slay's on Hampton was one restaurant where you would see a diverse crowd in the 1960s, and that was not common then. Everyone was welcome there."

Many people today still remember the rosin-baked potatoes served at Slay's. "We called them baked, but actually they were boiled in a pot with rosin, and then wrapped in butcher paper," recalls Slay. "The rosin coating kept the potatoes hot, and gave them a very subtle boost in aroma and flavor. People loved those potatoes." Another fond memory of the mayor's was watching his father walk among the tables and sing. "He has a great voice."

SINCE 1911

Slay recalls eating hummus at his dad's restaurant in the 1960s. "Hummus is everywhere now, but at Slay's you always got a free appetizer—hummus, three-bean salad, and beets, all served with Lebanese flatbread," says Slay. "We didn't close until 3 a.m. I helped out on weekends, and after we cleaned up, my dad and I would go to Schultz's Bakery about 4 a.m. and buy fresh doughnuts."

The Slay family also owned Slay's of Grantwood for twenty-two years, and they had Slay's Caruso's—a popular pizza place—on Manchester Road at Brentwood Boulevard. (The restaurant later moved north on Brentwood.) Slay's sister and brother-in-law, Sharon and Bill Bourne, and his brother Raymond operated Rick's Café Americain (later known as Raymond Slay's) in Shrewsbury. Another brother, Michael, serves as a chef on privately owned railway cars. David Slay, a cousin who now lives in California, owned several restaurants here and is said to have introduced flash-fried spinach to St. Louis.

Three generations of Lombardos have fed St. Louisans. In 1929, Augustus Lombardo opened a fruit stand in North St. Louis County. Five years later, customers dropping in to buy produce could also purchase spaghetti, ravioli, and sandwiches. In 1952, the Lombardo family put in a bigger kitchen to better accommodate their growing business. By 1964, the beefed-up fruit stand at Riverview and West Florissant Roads was replaced by a "real" restaurant.

Today, Carmine Lombardo and his daughter, Karen Baker, run Lombardo's Restaurant at 10488 Natural Bridge. Carmine's son Tony Lombardo is in charge of Lombardo's Trattoria at 201 South Twentieth Street, and Tony's brother Mike Lombardo can be found at Carmine's Steak House, at 20 South Fourth Street.

Some members of restaurant families get out of the kitchen and into a frying pan of a different sort—most notably, Mayor Francis G. Slay. "I can't cook," he says. In the late 1940s, Slay's grandfather, Joseph Slay, opened a barbecue place on Hampton Avenue that evolved into Slay's Restaurant, which later was owned by the mayor's father, Francis R. Slay, and two of his uncles, Mike and Anthony Slay. The restaurant closed in 1988.

Today, the mayor's father manages the Cedars Banquet Hall. His cousin Dennis Slay and Dennis's daughter Diana Slay own Zaytoon (that's "olive" in Lebanese) downtown, his cousin Lisa Slay cooks at Remy's Kitchen & Wine Bar in Clayton, and his cousins Jamie and Steve Komorek own Trattoria Marcella on Watson Road, named for their mother, who is Mayor Slay's aunt.

What cuisine does Slay favor? "I don't get to eat out often, but I like fish," he says. Slay also speaks highly of his Sicilian father-in-law's pasta dishes and risottos. "I am an adventurous eater, and I do like to try new things, go new places. It's great that we have so many restaurants in St. Louis."

WHAT MAKES A RESTAURANT "ETHNIC?"

The restaurants in a typical American city reflect the makeup of the population, and St. Louis is no exception. Our town is a rich mixture of restaurants that represent many cultures, all of them building individual cuisines on the basics—beef, chicken, pork, and fish—using spices and seasonings as dictated by family recipes from a faraway place. The French came first, and through the centuries, with each successive influx of immigrants, all of us who live here and eat here have benefited from exposure to other cuisines, all dubbed "ethnic" when we first encountered them. In 2008, most of us readily accept and embrace what we once considered different as simply part of the vibrant restaurant scene in the St. Louis area.

In the 1950s, immigrants from Italy, Greece, Germany, and Asia opened family restaurants. By the 1970s, mom-and-pop Chinese eateries had opened in many neighborhoods. Today, the Chinese Yellow Pages lists 250 Asian restaurants in the metropolitan area. When the Sunshine Inn opened in 1974 in the Central West End, the vegetarian fare was "foreign" to many customers, who also were annoyed that no coffee or alcohol were available.

That same year, Ramon Gallardo was making plans to open a Mexican restaurant at a time when the only Mexican restaurants in town were small mom-and-pop places with a half-dozen tables and no room for customers to socialize. Gallardo went to California to see El Torito, a chain with "beautiful buildings and good-looking food," and he went to Kansas City to look at Houlihan's, with its eclectic décor and stand-up tables in the bar.

"What I wanted was a Mexican Houlihan's, something cool, something different from a typical Mexican restaurant. No sombreros," says Gallardo, laughing. "I wanted Mexican art, Mexican antiques, Mexican fixtures—a casual place for people to be together." Another restaurateur told Gallardo to forget it, that his idea didn't have much of a chance for success.

Undaunted, Gallardo opened Casa Gallardo in Westport in 1975. Four years later, General Mills came courting and offered to help Gallardo build a chain of his restaurants. "That was the most phenomenal experience," he recalls. "I had not had the grooming for the job, and it took about a year to get familiar with being a subsidiary." Originally, General Mills wanted just one branch in each market, but over time they decided to copy the successful model established by Red Lobster and penetrate a market with numerous units.

"The idea was to open enough units in one market to pool resources and pay for television advertising," says Gallardo. "That was the beginning of chain expansion, and it changed the landscape of the restaurant industry." At its peak, the Casa Gallardo chain was in thirty-four locations—the third-largest chain of Mexican restaurants in the country—with seven restaurants here. Five remain open in the metropolitan area, all operated by a national firm. Gallardo is no longer involved with the restaurants but notes, "I'm very proud of what I did here."

After leaving General Mills, Gallardo had several successful restaurants. Among them was Ramon's Jalapeno in Clayton, where he introduced margaritas served in a shaker and ahi tuna, served medium rare. "I saw both of those in California," recalls Gallardo. "The margaritas were a super hit that made us different, but the tuna was considered weird at first," He laughs. "You want to be careful not to bring anything here too soon, because California usually is about four or five years ahead of us."

A native of Mexico City, Gallardo came to St. Louis in 1959. Before that, he had flirted with law school in Chicago but ended up working in the restaurant business. For thirteen years, he worked for Stephen Apted here and helped build Apted's La Sala into the first upscale Mexican restaurant in town. Today, Gallardo has Ozzie's Restaurant and Sports Bar in Westport and his wife, Ann, owns The City Coffee House and Creperie at 36 North Central in Clayton.

In the 1980s, St. Louisans actively sought out California cuisine—once considered suspect—and delighted in more opportunities to eat ethnic food, including soul food. Suddenly, neighborhoods all over town boasted restaurants specializing in French, Mexican, Japanese, Hungarian, Indian, and Middle Eastern fare. Tom Hsu cooked in St. Louis all through the 1980s, garnering rave reviews for his Hunan

Ramon Gallardo, full of hope for the future in this undated photo, opened his first restaurant in 1975. Courtesy of Missouri Restaurant Association.

dishes at a series of Chinese restaurants. Today, you'll find Hsu at the Hunan Star in Des Peres. By the late 1980s, Chinese buffets were opening in many a neighborhood, among them Lee and Jenny Pa's Happy China in Creve Coeur, where lunch and dinner come from the extensive buffet.

Pho Grand, a Vietnamese restaurant at 3195 South Grand that opened in 1989, serves as the anchor for that neighborhood's cultural stew of restaurants, which includes additional Vietnamese restaurants as well as eateries specializing in Persian, Ethiopian, Afghan, Thai, Chinese, and other cuisines. The 1990s brought us additional spots where we could dine on soul food and delicious dishes from Nepal, Bosnia, and Somalia. Mediterranean meals and Pacific Rim styles of cooking soon followed, and after that came "fusion"—an "old-is-new-again" culinary method that integrates regional cooking styles to create new tastes.

Steakhouses also made a comeback in the 1990s, and St. Louis County Executive Charlie Dooley is thankful for that. "I'm a steak and baked potato man," says Dooley, "and I like crumbled bacon on that potato." He lists some favorite dining spots, including Ruth's Chris Steak House, The Crossing, Busch's Grove, Fleming's Prime Steakhouse, Annie Gunn's, Dominic's Trattoria, and the Goody Goody Diner. "I know I'm leaving some out. It all depends on what you want to eat—there are a lot of great restaurants here."

In a truly democratic way, fusion cooking blurs the edges of ethnic cooking, introduces ingredients and cooking styles from one culture to ingredients and cooking styles of another—or two—and the result is almost always worthy.

Zoë Houk Robinson, who once wanted to be a fashion designer, embraced fusion early and often, even before many of us knew what it was. Robinson's interest in Asian food began in the early 1980s when she worked with several refugees from Laos. She was particularly impressed with the delicious food her new friends fixed themselves for lunch. "As soon as I opened my first restaurant, I hired as many of the Laotians as I could and I put a lot of their dishes on our menu." Ny Vongsaly has worked off and on as a chef for Robinson from the beginning.

That "beginning" was at Café Zoë, which Robinson opened in Lafayette Square in 1983, when she was twenty-three. "There was no money and I didn't know what I was doing. I just did it," she says. "I started working in restaurants when I was nineteen. It was the first thing I was really good at."

In 1990, Robinson moved Café Zoë to Clayton. "We grew up then," Robinson says. "We got a bigger place, expanded ourselves creatively, bought more equipment—we even had a real loan." After seven years, Robinson left Clayton and opened Zoë's Pan-Asian Café in the Central West End. That restaurant closed in October 2007. In 2001, Robinson returned to Clayton with I Fratellini. Robinson expected to launch her BoBo Noodle House in June 2008 on North Skinker Boulevard across from Washington University.

After twenty-five years, Robinson still likes being in the restaurant business in St. Louis. "There have always been sophisticated diners here, well educated and well traveled," she says. "I love my job."

THE GREAT PASTRAMI WAR

One of the well-loved restaurants here went to war in 1961—over pastrami.

First, some history: In the second half of the nineteenth century, Jewish immigrants brought pastrami from Eastern Europe, where pastrami was a signature dish of several local cuisines. Later—much later—it was a signature dish in St. Louis at Kopperman's, established in 1897; Protzel's, in business since 1954; the Posh Nosh, which opened in 1966; and at Jack Carl's 2 Cents Plain, which originally opened at 4263 Olive, in Gaslight Square. (For more on Gaslight Square, see Chapter 5.)

"We rented a spot between two bars, the Golden Eagle and the Opera House, and we were doing well," recalls Carl. "By 1961, the owners wanted me out so they could have the building—and that was the beginning of the Great Pastrami Wars."

Carl was selling huge pastrami sandwiches—served with pickles and a knish—for one dollar. The building owners hired away one of Carl's employees and started selling pastrami sandwiches for seventy-five cents. Carl lowered his prices to match that, and then the bars

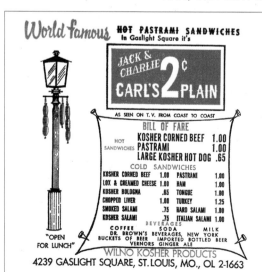

World famous HOT PASTRAMI SANDWICHES
In Gaslight Square it's

JACK & CHARLIE
CARL'S 2¢ PLAIN

AS SEEN ON T.V. FROM COAST TO COAST

BILL OF FARE

HOT SANDWICHES
KOSHER CORNED BEEF 1.00
PASTRAMI 1.00
LARGE KOSHER HOT DOG .65

COLD SANDWICHES
KOSHER CORNED BEEF 1.00   PASTRAMI 1.00
LOX & CREAMED CHEESE 1.00   HAM 1.00
KOSHER BOLOGNA .85   TONGUE 1.00
CHOPPED LIVER 1.00   TURKEY 1.25
SMOKED SALAMI .75   HARD SALAMI 1.00
KOSHER SALAMI .75   ITALIAN SALAMI 1.00

BEVERAGES
COFFEE   SODA   MILK
DR. BROWN'S BEVERAGES, NEW YORK
BUCKETS OF BEER   IMPORTED BOTTLED BEER
VERNORS GINGER ALE

"OPEN FOR LUNCH"

WILNO KOSHER PRODUCTS
4239 GASLIGHT SQUARE, ST. LOUIS, MO., OL 2-1663

dropped their prices to fifty cents. The Pastrami War made national headlines, and newspaper columnist and book author Harry Golden included the story in one of his books.

What happened next?

"When people found out what was going on, my business came back, but the building owners sued to evict me," says Carl. "I had helped out at the bar next door from time to time, so I went to court and told the judge that the bar owner was watering down the whisky. I also said that I had been instructed to save all the old coffee for Irish coffee drinks." Carl grins at the memory. "The judge said they couldn't evict me."

Once he'd won the war, Carl triumphantly moved down the street. His older brother, Charlie, closed his deli in University City and joined Jack at 4239 Olive, where they again sold "World Famous Pastrami Sandwiches" for a dollar. They kept the name—2 Cents Plain—which

Jack and Charlie Carl's 2 Cents Plain was a popular eatery in Gaslight Square. Courtesy of Jack Carl.

Carl says is a reference to the days when you could get a large glass of plain seltzer for two cents. Flavoring cost another penny.

In 1969, Carl left Gaslight Square. In 1971, he opened on Eleventh Street downtown, where the walls were covered with pictures and posters, and shelves displayed bowling trophies, bottle collections, and campaign buttons. After twenty years there, Carl moved to 1114 Olive, where he spent another twenty years.

Through the years, people came to 2 Cents Plain for the pastrami, but they also came to experience Carl's unusual brand of hospitality. Carl yelled at his customers, a gimmick he adapted from Carnegie's and Stages, famous delis in New York City. "Waiters at those delis would say, 'Give me your order—I don't have all day,'" recalls Carl. "If you asked to split one of the big sandwiches, the waiters would say that costs an extra four dollars. I decided to bring that style of service here, to be different. I only yelled at people I knew."

Retired since 2005, Carl now works part-time at the deli at Straub's in the Central West End, which he says is a "Have a Nice Day" kind of place. "You are supposed to be extra nice," says Carl. "One judge I know came over and asked me why I was not yelling at him, so I did. Once in a while, I love upsetting the courtesy applecart at Straub's."

You don't hear much about the Pastrami War any more today, but one way to start an argument is to declare any given pizza place the best in St. Louis. Everybody has an opinion, and those opinions seem to carry more weight when expressed in a loud voice. Here are some places that garner repeated shouts of approval: Joe Boccardi's, Balducci's, Caito's, Cicero's, Dewey's, Farotto's, Feraro's Jersey Style Pizza, j j twig's, Fortel's, Frank & Helen's, Pi, Racanelli's, and Vito's. A new pizza place earning high marks is Katie's Pizzeria Café in Clayton, owned by twenty-six-year-old Katie Lee, Zoë Robinson's niece.

THE SQUARE BEYOND COMPARE

And then there is Imo's Pizza, the longtime hometown favorite. Eight million Imo's pizzas are sold each year, made in ninety-five locations. Marge and Ed Imo never imagined their little idea would grow into something so big. In 1964, the couple lived on the Hill with their two children. Ed was a tile setter's helper, looking for a better job. The Imos had a goal. They wanted to make $10,000 a year so they could buy a house.

"On Friday nights, we'd order a pizza from one of the restaurants nearby, and Ed would go pick it up," recalls Marge Imo.

Imo's pizza is a tradition in St. Louis. Courtesy of Imo's.

"We'd sit there in the kitchen, eating the pizza, and talk about how great it would be to have a pizza brought to us. There was a place on Hampton that delivered chicken—why not pizza? We decided we'd open a little place that delivered pizza."

The couple had saved $1,500. They bought an oven, two refrigerators, a stove, a counter, and pizza pans, all used. They rented an eight hundred-square-foot storefront on Thurman and Shaw. They didn't have a cash register, so Ed cleaned out one of his fishing tackle boxes. "Then we just did it—we told all our friends, and we opened the first Imo's Pizza," says Imo. "I answered the phone and took orders, Ed made the pizzas, and my brother delivered them. A month later, we hired a real pizza maker named Vic, and Ed helped with deliveries."

The business grew, first from word of mouth and then with a little help from some flyers that the Imos distributed in the neighborhood. Six months later, some close friends said they wanted to get into the business, so the Imos opened a second store at 3210 California with their friends as partners. "Then we opened another one, and another—our first fifteen stores all were operated by friends or family, but eventually we had to franchise," Imo says.

Initially reluctant to open in St. Charles because it seemed so far away, the Imos relented when an entire neighborhood in that community submitted a petition promising that every family would buy at least one pizza a week. "When we opened in Webster, people in Kirkwood called to say they wanted an Imo's. Early on, we didn't ever think we could really be big," says Imo. Suddenly, we had forty stores, and we asked ourselves, 'How did that happen?'"

At the request of customers, the Imos added soft drinks to their menu. Then they added salads. After much discussion, they agreed to add chicken wings, which turned out to be big sellers. Eventually, the Imos even added tables and chairs. "Our niche was always carry-out and delivery," says Imo. "We do it well."

Today, all six of the couple's children are in the family business. Ed—who likes sausage, mushrooms, and onions on his pizza—makes store visits several times a week. Marge (hold the mushrooms on hers) works a couple of days a week in the company's office, which is on the Hill. The couple now owns a company that makes the pizza shells, grinds the meat, bakes the bread, and makes the sauce and salad dressing for the restaurants.

The most popular pizza at Imo's is sausage, the one that the Imos started with in 1964. "We just wanted to make a good living, and we've done that. We try to give good value for good food, and we've also been able to provide a lot of good jobs for a lot of wonderful people. Also, we've been able to help support local charities," says Imo. "I'm proud of St. Louis and I'm proud of Imo's Pizza."

Another local restaurant owner has achieved great success opening one place, and then repeating the formula again and again, building a chain of restaurants, link by link. That chain is The Pasta House Co., owned by J. Kim Tucci and Joe Fresta. Currently, there are thirty-one Pasta House restaurants (some are franchises) and four Pronto! locations (the smaller sibling) in the metropolitan area.

THE PASTA HOUSE CO.

With that kind of success, Tucci and Fresta can sit back and relax, right?

Wrong. They work hard to reflect changing tastes. Their menus offer low-fat and low-carb dishes, as well as whole wheat pasta. Earlier this year, Tucci was putting together a new lasagna recipe. "I've got more ideas than ever," says Tucci. Seated in The Pasta House Co. on Delmar at Bonhomme, he points

to a nearby wall. "That was the eastern wall of the first Pasta House, which was eight hundred square feet."

Then Tucci explains the genealogy of his popular chain. Rich Ronzio and Charlie Mugavero already owned a Jewish-Italian deli when they decided in 1969 to start a restaurant. John Ferrara joined the partnership, and they opened Rich and Charlie's Trattoria on Oakland just east of Hampton Avenue, forever changing how St. Louis thinks about salad and introducing us to pasta con broccoli. Later, two of Ronzio's nephews opened a second Rich and Charlie's in South St. Louis County.

A year later, Ronzio and Mugavero—with Tucci, Fresta, Marty Ronzio, and Emil Pozzo on board—opened Rich and Charlie's in Ballwin. In 1973, Mugavero was killed in a plane crash. The owners decided to change the name to The Pasta House Co., and they opened a restaurant downtown. In 1978, Rich Ronzio was bought out, as were Ronzio's nephews, who still operate Rich and Charlie's in several locations. Ferrara, Fresta, and Tucci started expanding and growing. Ferrara died in 2001.

"Today, The Pasta House Co. serves five million people a year, which makes us the largest local 'feeder' in Missouri," says

Joe Fresta and J. Kim Tucci have built The Pasta House Co. empire. Courtesy of The Pasta House Co.

WOMEN IN THE KITCHEN: TEN HONOREES

In 1998, ten women were honored as Women of Achievement by the St. Louis branch of the Missouri Restaurant Association. Selected by their peers for "contributing to the positive image of the restaurant industry through their business ethics and leadership," the women had more than 250 years in the business among them at the time.

Today, all but three remain in the business. Here's to women in the kitchen!

Mary Hostetter
The Blue Owl

Karen Duffy
Duff's

Simone Andujar
Malmaison

Jan Yacovelli
Yacovelli's

Zoë Robinson
Zoë's Pan Asian

Giovanna Bruno
Bruno's of Little Italy

Mary Rose Del Pietro
Del Pietro's

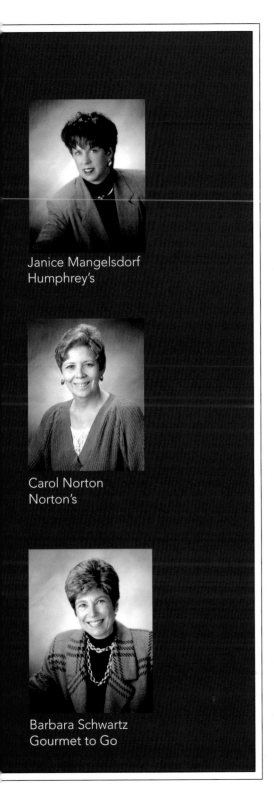

Janice Mangelsdorf
Humphrey's

Carol Norton
Norton's

Barbara Schwartz
Gourmet to Go

Tucci. He is proud of that. Tucci also is proud that he established "selling seminars" for his employees that he says "changed the culture of this company." And Tucci is proud that The Pasta House Co. got McMurphy's Grill, at 614 North Eleventh Street, up and running.

Opened by the St. Patrick Center in 1990, McMurphy's Grill was the first full-service restaurant in the country dedicated to providing food-service training for homeless and individuals who are mentally disabled. The Boeing Foundation and the Boeing Employees Community Fund provided start-up funding, Paul and Midge McKee donated the location for McMurphy's to the St. Patrick Center, and The Pasta House Co. set up and implemented an early training program, and they also donated kitchen equipment.

Today, Anheuser-Busch Companies, Inc., and the Boeing Foundation help underwrite the costs of the restaurant training program, which allows thirty to forty people to embark on careers in the restaurant industry each year. "Helping McMurphy's was a great experience, and McMurphy's is a great legacy for Edith Cunnane, the superstar who first had the idea," says Tucci. (That "superstar" is a philanthropist and activist who founded St. Patrick Center over twenty-five years ago.)

Fast-food chains also have a presence in St. Louis. White Castle claims to be the first fast-food hamburger chain. J. Walter Anderson, who attended college in Sedalia, Missouri, opened the first White Castle in Wichita, Kansas, in 1921. According to David Hogan's book *Selling 'Em by the Sack,* the first White Castle in the St. Louis area opened in 1925 on South Eighteenth Street. At one time, St. Louis was the biggest market for the chain, with eighteen restaurants here. In 1958, Don Kuehl and Bill Wyatt opened the first local McDonald's, in Crestwood.

The Pasta House Co. welcomes families. Courtesy of The Pasta House Co.

SERIAL RESTAURATEURS

For some restaurant owners, satisfaction comes from perfecting one place and then developing a second concept at a different location. Wendy and Paul Hamilton own two places: Eleven Eleven Mississippi (guess where?) and Vin de Set at 2017 Chouteau.

Eleven Eleven Mississippi, a wine country bistro spread over five thousand square feet, opened in December 2003. "Our timing was right, and we nailed a lot of things," says Paul Hamilton. "We were lucky." The couple also had complementary backgrounds. Wendy knew marketing; Paul knew restaurants. Today, the Hamiltons get a lot of credit for the rebirth of the northern side of Lafayette Square.

In June 2006, the Hamiltons opened Vin de Set in a building that once served as a mill for the Schnaider Brewery. A thirty thousand-square-foot restaurant, Vin de Set specializes in casual southern French cuisine. "We've got a restaurant on the roof, banquet space, and a rental space on the first floor," says Hamilton. "It's bigger than we'd planned, but now that it's done, I'm glad we did it."

Hamilton is optimistic about the restaurant scene in St. Louis. "There is a lot of talent here, a lot of variety, and the proximity of restaurants here is good," he says. "In some towns, it's harder to restaurant-hop. Here, no matter where you live, you can find nice variety—and for the price, eating in St. Louis is the best value anywhere."

Before Paul and Wendy Hamilton opened their restaurants, Paul worked for Tim Mallett, another man who started with one place. Now there are three: Remy's Kitchen & Wine Bar in Clayton, Blue Water Grill in Kirkwood, and Big Sky Café in Webster Groves. "Remy's was thirteen in February, Big Sky was sixteen in April, and Blue Water Grill will be twenty years old in November," sums up Mallett, "and those years go quickly in a 24/7 type of business."

Mallett adds that he is well aware of the vagaries of the restaurant business, where "one man's fiery bowl of chili is over-spiced for someone else," but he says his customers tell him

Top: Customers enjoy drinks at the bar at Vin de Set, 2017 Chouteau Avenue. Courtesy of Vin de Set.

Above: Eleven Eleven Mississippi boasts a lovely patio. Courtesy of Eleven Eleven Mississippi.

ST. LOUIS ORIGINALS: KEEPING IT LOCAL

Sixty percent of restaurants in the metropolitan area are independently owned and operated. In 2003, some of them banded together "to unite the energies of local restaurants and to celebrate the food and friendship that's indigenous to St. Louis neighborhoods."

Paul Hamilton, current president of the St. Louis Originals, says that mission is more important now than ever. "When you eat at independently owned restaurants, your money stays here. You're not sending it to some corporate headquarters in another city," he says.

Member restaurants also support more than five hundred area charities, causes, and events, donating more than $1 million every year in cash, gift certificates, labor, food, and gifts.

More than twenty-five thousand area residents have signed up for the St. Louis Originals Rewards Card, which earns diners points that can be applied to meals at member restaurants. For more information, see www.stlouisoriginals.com. Membership, which is free, also entitles diners to purchase gift cards and discounted web certificates for favorite restaurants.

About forty restaurants, cafés, and caterers are members of the St. Louis Originals. "That number changes as restaurants open and close," says Hamilton, who with his wife, Wendy, owns Eleven Eleven Mississippi and Vin de Set. "As the organization moves into the future, we're looking at how to raise our value to the community." Originals include:

Baileys' Chocolate Bar
Bryan Young Catering Plus
Cafe Provencal
Companion Bakehouses
Copia
Cravings Restaurant and Bakery
Cunetto House of Pasta
Delmar Lounge
Dierdorf & Harts
Duff's
Eau
Eleven Eleven Mississippi
Farotto's
The Gramophone
Harry's Restaurant & Bar
Harvest
Juniper Grill
LoRusso's Cucina
Massa's

Mike Shannon's
Monarch
Off the Vine
Ricardo's Italian Cafe
Riddle's Penultimate Cafe
Rooster
Savor
Schlafly Tap Room/Bottleworks
Serendipity Ice Cream
Soda Fountain Square
Square One Brewery
SqWires Restaurant and Market
Sunset 44 Bistro
Tenderloin Room
Terrene
The Gardens at Malmaison
Trattoria Marcella
Villa Farotto
Vin de Set
Wild Horse Grill

that great food and great service at a fair price is the magic formula. "It sounds simple, but getting all the stars and moons and gods to align at the same time is a challenge every day, but when it works, it's motivating on a personal level."

Making it work in multiple locations is a challenge, Mallett admits, but lessons learned at one restaurant can be applied at the others. One problem for every restaurant owner in town is the constant influx of new places to eat.

"Because we have been established for several years, we have had time to develop some loyal patrons, but new restaurants are striving for attention in a very competitive market," says Mallett. "Getting someone to pick your new restaurant more than once is a challenge, when so many are vying for every customer's attention."

FLYING SOLO

Thom Sehnert, owner of Annie Gunn's in Chesterfield, reports that within the last four years, four thousand restaurant seats opened within one mile of his place. "And yet," Sehnert notes wryly, "we had our best year ever in 2007." Accordingly, Sehnert and his wife, Jane, have no plans to open another restaurant. "Annie Gunn's is my one and only," says Sehnert. "I'd rather have one very good restaurant and concentrate on that."

The Smokehouse Market is next to the restaurant. There, the Sehnerts sell gourmet meats, imported and domestic cheeses, fresh produce and a variety of condiments. "We bought the store in 1980 thinking we would complement what groceries do and add a European-style butcher," recalls Sehnert. "We went to the bank, and the loan officer remarked that no one

Tim Mallett (inset) feeds St. Louisans at his Blue Water Grill (top), Remy's Kitchen & Wine Bar (right), and Big Sky Café. Courtesy of Tim Mallett.

ERIC BRENNER AND MIKE JOHNSON:
ON THE RESTAURANT SCENE

Eric Brenner

Mike Johnson

Energy drives the restaurant business, a focused passion that ideally flows from the owner/chef to every staff member and on to every customer seated at every table in the dining room. Eric Brenner, thirty-eight, and Mike Johnson, thirty-seven, possess that energy, and both have greatly influenced the local restaurant scene.

Brenner, owner of Moxy Contemporary Bistro in the Central West End, has cooked at or consulted for Chez Leon, Sub Zero Vodka Bar, Araka, Lucas Park Grill, Flannery's, Kaldi's Coffeehouses, The Bistro at Grand Center, Z, Truffles, the Ritz-Carlton Hotel, the Racquet Club-Ladue, and the St. Louis Country Club.

Johnson's newest restaurant is Fumanchu, a pan-Asian place in Maplewood specializing in dim sum and sushi. With Carey McDowell and Charlie Downs, Johnson also is part of Revival at Thirty-Ninth Street and Chouteau. With other partners, Johnson owns BARcelona Tapas, Momos, Boogaloo, Roxane, and El Scorcho. He helped open Cyrano's in Webster Groves and he headed up the now defunct Figaro and Café Mira.

moxy
contemporary bistro

That last was Johnson's first. Opened in 1996, Café Mira was a fine dining restaurant in Clayton that specialized in contemporary American cuisine. Johnson has moved away from that concept—far away. "When you are younger, you want to make a statement, bring something new to town, do something no one has ever done," says Johnson. "Now I go for places with a cool atmosphere and really good food that is easy to prepare."

Brenner understands that. "I always say to younger chefs that their key ingredient should be humility. There are a lot of great chefs in town who know tons more than you do when you start out," says Brenner. "So I tell them it's never about you. It's about the people who come to you. If you have something unique, good for you—that may keep you in business, but it will not ensure success."

Conceding that owning a restaurant is a hard business, Brenner still describes himself as an optimist. "We're in a war, we're in a recession, debt is skyrocketing—but I still think it's critical that we create more 'food scenes,' have groups of restaurants in neighborhoods," he says. "On our corner in the Central West End, the restaurants huddle together, work together, and keep our corner in the press. The emphasis is collective collaboration, not individual competition."

That said, Brenner thinks there are too many restaurants in town, and Johnson agrees. "I had to wait months—almost a year—to get liquor licenses to open a BARcelona Tapas in Indianapolis and Cincinnati, and each license cost me over fifty thousand dollars," he says. "In St. Louis, you take a note from your mom and $400 and you get a license right away."

The burgeoning number of restaurants here has not resulted in diminished quality. "Compared to other cities our size," Johnson says, "St. Louis is ten levels above all of them when it comes to great places to eat."

COOKING UP RESTAURANT SPACE

Restaurant people have vision and courage. Some open up in a typical restaurant space. Others see tables, chairs, and happy customers dining in surprising spaces that are anything but typical. They transform—and then manage to transcend—places with myriad former uses. Local foodie and raconteur Doug Travis compiled this list:

- Chevy's in Olivette is in a Quonset hut that used to be the home of Ladue Local Lines, a school bus company.

- Eleven Eleven Mississippi took over an old shoe factory.

- Fitz's in University City is in a former bank, as was First Federal Frank and Crust, a defunct pizza place in Clayton.

- The old Joe and Charlie's in Richmond Heights once was a flower shop.

- The Granary, a bar in Edwardsville, was in a grain elevator.

- Grappa (and several restaurants since) opened in the Central West End in a Pierce-Arrow automobile dealership.

- Hacienda in Overland is in a former Western Auto store.

- O'Brien's in Richmond Heights was in an old Uniroyal tire store.

- Savor in the Central West End is in a former funeral home, as was the departed ZuZu's Petals in Kirkwood.

- SqWires in Lafayette Square is in the old Western Wire Factory complex.

- Trailhead Brewing Company in St. Charles is in an old grist mill.

Bevo Mill. Courtesy of Robbi Courtaway.

- Zinnia in Webster Groves was in a refurbished gas station.

St. Louisans also like to eat on boats—the *Robert E. Lee* and the *Belle Angeline* come to mind. Noah's Ark, a longtime landmark in St. Charles, was built to look like a particular boat. The old Bayou Belle also was a boat look-a-like. The Bevo Mill, at 4749 Gravois, has always looked just like what it is—a windmill—built as a restaurant in 1915 for August A. Busch, Sr.

was eating red meat anymore. We argued that when they do, they want the best cut available, and they would come to a butcher shop."

In 1990, the Sehnerts built Annie Gunn's. "The idea was to take the fresh ingredients we sold at the store and offer the same cuisine, freshly prepared," says Sehnert. He named the restaurant for his great-grandmother. "She was a gracious Irish lady with no money, but her house was always full of people and a lot of food. We liked that theme, staying true to our roots."

In 1993, a memorable flood roared through Missouri, and when it was all over, water from the Missouri River had risen thirteen feet high in the Sehnerts' low-lying restaurant and store. "The only thing we had left was the skeleton of the brick building, but we decided to grow where we were planted, and we rebuilt, with no regrets," he says. Construction of a levee said to hold back even a flood of the magnitude of that of 1993 comforts the Sehnerts.

Another comfort is their staff of 130, led by Chef Lou Rook (who was nominated for Best Chef in the Midwest by the James Beard Society) and their wine guru, Glenn Bardgett. "What you get at Annie Gunn's is an honest plate of great, straightforward food," says Sehnert. "We love what we do, and we hope it shows."

Another restaurateur happy with one place and one place only is Karen Duffy, co-owner with Tim Kirby of Duff's in the Central West End. Duffy opened the restaurant on July 7, 1972, with one thousand dollars, a credit card, and a lot of help from friends.

"Before we opened, we were knocking out plaster to expose the brick and painting, and people would come by and ask what we were doing. We'd tell them, and they would offer to help," recalls Duffy. "One woman gave us a refrigerator, another gave us some extra forks, one brought in a table, and we got a lot of furniture from Goodwill."

The kitchen was already in place, as the building had once housed Jimmy Aumon's Tea Room, a formal eatery. Before opening, Duffy

ORVILLE MIDDENDORF:
STAKING IT ALL ON STEAK

Orville Middendorf knows the meat business. For forty years, he owned and operated Middendorf Meat Company, which distributes meat, seafood, and canned foods to restaurants, hotels, clubs, and hospitals. From the beginning, the company has specialized in custom-cut steaks.

Though he is now retired, Middendorf still talks about the business with pride. "I started in the meat business when I was fourteen years old. I worked for two small meat companies, where I learned quality levels, and then I went in the service," Middendorf recalls. "When I came home, I went to work selling meat for a company, and I did well. At one point I figured if I could do this for someone else, I could do it for myself."

In 1962, Middendorf decided that St. Louis needed a meat company that handled only choice and prime meats. He started small, with just four thousand dollars and a handful of customers. (Steve Apted was one of them.) Middendorf rented a small storefront. He bought a used cooler and some equipment from a grocery that had gone out of business. He built a walk-in cooler.

"At this point I had a wife and a baby, so I went to work at Kroger's meat counter nights and weekends while I got my company going during the day," Middendorf says. "Fortunately, I was accepted quickly, and I knew it was just a matter of time before I could grow the company."

Originally, Middendorf bought sides of beef. "Then the industry changed," he says. As a member of the National Association of Meat Purveyors, Middendorf visited packing houses where steaks were cut to order and then shipped in boxes to distributors. He also attended seminars on innovative techniques for aging meat, sponsored by the U.S. Department of Agriculture. "I was always learning something new about the business."

For twenty years, Middendorf sold only meat. In 1982, he expanded his business to include grocery products. By 2002, Middendorf had grown significantly. "We had $100 million in sales, and suddenly everybody wanted to buy the company," he says. "I sold it to Performance Food Group after they promised they would not let go even a single one of my two hundred employees. They kept that promise, and they have maintained the original name and the reputation for quality."

Today, Middendorf serves as a consultant for the company he founded. He is involved with several charitable organizations and institutions. He sits on a handful of corporate boards, as well as the board of L'Ecole Culinaire, and he is active with the St. Louis Chefs de Cuisine Association. He also is associated with hospitality studies and culinary arts programs at St. Louis Community College at Forest Park and Southwestern Illinois College in Granite City.

Where does Middendorf like to have dinner?

"A little place called Roberto's, which has terrific Italian food," he says. "And I think Al's is the best steakhouse there ever was."

Diners enjoy the patio at Duffs in the Central West End. Courtesy of Duff's.

polled her helpers about what job titles they preferred. Gene Smith, who worked at Bill Burgdorf's bookstore around the corner and had cooked for the Pulitzer family from time to time, helped set up the menu. Ginger Carlson Mostov, a caterer, worked as the executive chef. Former staffers from Jimmy Aumon signed on, members of a commune in Lafayette Square rotated shifts, and a number of otherwise unemployed Vietnam veterans also helped out.

The Days & Nights of the Central West End (Second Edition) describes the early days of Duff's: "When it opened, the furnishings consisted of mismatched auction specials, paintings good and bad covered the walls, and the ceiling was purple. Music was played some evenings, and the environment was pretty relaxed."

Prior to owning a restaurant, Duffy and her husband at the time, Dan Duffy, had traveled around Europe with their two children in a touring bus. "We'd eat at little neighborhood restaurants where people would go for a meal and to see one another, and we decided we'd like to open one," recalls Duffy. The couple lived in Chicago at the time, but on the flight home from Europe, they met someone who suggested the Central West End would be a perfect location for what they had in mind.

Over the years, Duffy invented two dishes: The early version of Duff's salad (originally based on a salad from Marshall Field's in Chicago) and the surprise burger. What was in the surprise

burger? "It was a surprise," says Duffy, laughing. She notes that every chef has served to inspire the next. Jimmy Voss, the current executive chef, started at Duff's in the mid-1970s as a dishwasher. "One day Jimmy was called on to chop an onion or something, and he showed an interest in food," she says.

Today, Duff's is noted for its great food, neighborly atmosphere, and poetry readings on Monday night, first established by Dan Duffy. "The poetry readings here are huge," says Duffy. "River Styx has organized the readings for thirty-three years now. We've had so many magical evenings—I've filled twelve scrapbooks."

By the way, the "new room" at Duff's is now eighteen years old. "I look back and think how fast time flies, and how the restaurant is always growing and changing," says Duffy. All this has been accomplished without a concept or a business plan or market studies. "We are what we are," says Duffy. What does the future hold for Duff's? Duffy laughs.

"Like that burger, it will be a surprise."

The same can be said for the St. Louis restaurant scene, where every day, in many a neighborhood, chefs are cooking up something delicious to tempt our collective palate.

SPEAKING OF RESTAURANTS: A LITANY OF GOOD FOOD

Ask people to rattle off favorite restaurants past and present, and some names are mentioned repeatedly. For instance:

Adriana's
Al's
Al Smith's
Almond's
Al-Tarboush Deli
Angelo's
Bartolino's
Bentley's
Black Cat
Black Forest
Blue Moon
Bobby's Creole
Boedecker's
The Branding Iron
Broadway Oyster Bar
Busy Bee Tea Room
Café de France
Café Hampton
Candlelight House
Catfish and Crystal
Chalet de Normandie
Charlotte's Rib
Chuy's
Cicardi's
City Diner
Coal Hole
The Coffee Pot
Cork and Cleaver
The Cottage
Creve Coeur Inn
The Crossing
The Crossroads
Cunetto House of Pasta
Dean Sisters
DeBergerac's
Dierdorf & Hart's
Dohack's
Dunie's
Eberhard's
Ed's White Front

Edmond's
Eisele's Black Forest
El Serape
Fio's La Fourchette
Flaming Pit
Flavor of India
Forum Cafeteria
Franco's
Garavelli's
Grecian Garden
Green Parrot Inn
The Greek Gourmet
Grone's Cafeteria
Harvest
Hatfield and McCoy's
Hendrickson's Cafeteria
The Hitching Post
Hodak's
House of India
House of Maret
House of Wong
Hunan Star
Iron Barley
Jackie's Place
Jefferson Avenue
    Boarding House
Jeremiah's
Jimmy's on the Park
Johnny's Seven-Mile House
Kemoll's
L'Auberge Bretonne
The Ladle
The Lantern House
La Sala
La Veranda
The Leather Bottle
Lee's Chinese Restaurant
Lemmon's
The Lettuce Leaf
Little Italy

Lotus Room
Louis IX
Madam de Foe's
Magic Pan
Mama Leone's
Manila Café
Mare's
The Mikado
Mr. D's West
Musial & Biggie's
Nantucket Cove
Noah's Ark
Odorizzi's
The Orient
The Original
Pagliacci's
Painted Pig
Painted Plates
Parente's
Parkmoor
Pat's Bar & Grill
Patrick's
Pavot
The Pelican
Phil's Barbecue
Pope's Cafeteria
Pond Inn
Port St. Louis
Pueblo Solis
R.L. Steamer's
Rail Fence Drive In
Ramelkamp's
Red Brick
Red Cedar Inn
Redel's
Rinaldi's
Roma's
Romaine's
Ruggeri's on the Hill
Ruiz
Sala's
The Salad Bowl
Saleem's
Sam the Watermelon Man

Sameem Afghan Restaurant
Sam's Steakhouse
Schneidhorst's Drive In
Schober's
Schumacher's
Shakey's Pizza
Shanghai Café
Sidney Street Café
Smokey Joe's Grecian Terrace
Smugala's
Soulard's
Sportsman's Park
Steiny's Inn
Stix Tearoom
Stradivarius
The Sun
Tack Room
Talayna's
Thompson's Cafeteria
Teutenberg's
Three Fountains
Toddle House
Top of the 230
Top of the Mark
Top of the Sevens
Trader Vic's
Uncle Bill's
Urban Restaurant
Vic's Barbecue
Webster Grill
White Horse Inn
Zia's
Zimfel's

Chapter 2

MADE IN ST. LOUIS:
LOCAL FOOD MANUFACTURERS

World-class salami and prosciutto. Spicy lentil dips. Fruit-flavored sorbets and rich gelatos. Salty pretzels twisted into surprising shapes. Sassy salsas. Celebrated hand-crafted chocolates. Red-hot potato chips. Mouth-watering pastries ranging from small buttery cookies to towering four-tiered cakes decorated with fresh flowers. Chewy red licorice. Craft breads made with old-world integrity.

Courtesy of SweetArt

Above: Reine Bayoc's shortbread cookie sandwiches are filled with caramel cream.

Previous Page: Giovanni Volpi (second from left) and other salami makers practice their culinary craft at the Volpi factory on the Hill in 1906. Courtesy of Volpi Foods.

All these flavorful foods—and many, many more—are produced right here in the metropolitan area. Over two hundred companies, large and small, manufacture food products that account for more than $2.5 billion in annual sales and shipments. So says a study released in 2007 by the St. Louis Agribusiness Club.

Where can you buy food products made in St. Louis and elsewhere in the state? Dierbergs, Schnucks, and Straub's all carry some local products, and Local Harvest Grocery on Morganford specializes in just that. (See Chapter 3 for information on local groceries.) Farmers' markets, of course, are perfect sources for locally grown and produced foods. (See Chapter 4.) And Missouri Mercantile, a store at St. Louis Mills in Hazelwood, carries food, wine, and gift items all made in Missouri. (Read more about Missouri wines in Chapter 5.)

Some local food producers opened for business over one hundred years ago. Some started up this summer, like Reine Bayoc, who opened SweetArt at 2203 South Thirty-Ninth Street in the Shaw Neighborhood in June 2008. The small retail shop carries Bayoc's made-from-scratch Moon Day Soul Treats (cookies, cupcakes, shortbread, brownies, and cakes) plus paintings by her husband, Cbabi Bayoc.

On World Environment Day in June 2005, Jessica Prentice, from the San Francisco Bay Area, gave the world a word for consumers who favor eating food grown and produced within a hundred-mile radius of their homes. The word is *locavore*. In 2007, the *New Oxford American Dictionary* chose it as Word of the Year.

SweetArt!
from-scratch bakeshop & art boutique

"I hope that takes off here," says Josh Allen, owner of Companion, which specializes in craft breads and pastries. "Bread and everything else is heading into an era of hyper-localization, with people wanting to buy locally. This is a good time to be a local brewer or baker or coffee roaster."

Local brewers have their say in Chapter 5. Among the local coffee-roasting companies are Kaldi's Coffee Roasting Company and Ronnoco Coffee Company. When Suzanne Langlois and Howard Lerner opened Kaldi's Coffeehouse at 700 DeMun Avenue in 1994, the owners started producing their own brew. The only certified organic coffee roasted in the area, Kaldi's coffee is now sold in local groceries and served in restaurants and at all six of the Kaldi's Cafés.

Legend has it that the O'Connor brothers first tasted roasted imported coffee beans at the 1904 World's Fair. They flipped the letters in their last name and went into the business, making deliveries in a horse-drawn buggy to local hotels. Said to be the largest coffee roaster in the area, Ronnoco's now sells to restaurants, hotels, and private clubs in seven states, and their Wildhorse Creek Coffee is available in many coffee houses.

Many a local neighborhood is filled with the soul-satisfying aroma of baking bread. St. Louis has it all: Dark pumpernickel, crusty Italian, braided challah, whole wheat, French, rosemary and olive, multigrain, tzizel rye, sourdough, cornbread, sunflower honey wheat, cracked pepper and Parmesan, handmade bagels, and even loaves with spinach and roasted red pepper baked in with a bit of Asiago cheese. At Black Bear Bakery, the bakers stir in a pinch of politics.

In other words, if you're interested in living on bread alone, this is the place.

BARBARA OLWIG: SELLING MISSOURI

Courtesy of Missouri Mercantile

Foods, books, art, wine, gift baskets, personal care products, and pet treats—all made in Missouri—fill the shelves at Missouri Mercantile, a shop tucked in the St. Louis Mills mall in Hazelwood. Owner Barbara Olwig, who lives in Florissant, proudly declares that about 15 percent of the shop's merchandise is made in the St. Louis area.

Food producers at the shop that are made in the metropolitan area include:

- Carla's St. Louis Vinegar
- Dad's Cookie Company
- Fat Pat's Seasonings
- Florence's HomeStyle Cha-Cha
- Gibbons Honey Products
- Happy Dogs Hot Sauce
- Little Pleasures Soups and Dips
- My House Salt
- Randy's Famous Salsa

Barbara and her husband, Bill Olwig, are longtime enthusiasts of locally produced food products. They have enjoyed attending the annual Best of Missouri market held at the Missouri Botanical Garden, she says. "We also like to visit Missouri wineries, and to stop in at antique stores and shops in small Missouri towns."

Over the years, the couple met vendors with interesting products to sell. One day, Bill, who works in construction, suggested Barbara open a store that pays tribute to foods and gift items made in Missouri. In October 2002, Missouri Mercantile: Purveyors of Fine Missouri Products opened in an historic building in downtown Florissant. A year later, St. Louis Mills came courting, and now the shop is in the mall.

"We get a lot of compliments on the store," Olwig notes. "And our customers always say they feel good supporting the little guy, supporting Missourians."

That was not always the case. According to *Our Missouri: Foods*, a brochure published in 1992 by Missouri Interpretive Materials, one of the first large bakeries in the Louisiana Territory was in St. Louis, but that didn't mean bread was plentiful. In those days, farmers brought grain to the mill, and in return for services rendered, the miller kept some of the flour, which he then traded to the baker in exchange for fresh bread.

Over time, St. Louis came to be called *paincourt*, a French term that meant "short of bread," because merchants simply could not keep up with the demand.

THE STAFF OF LIFE

Charlie Fazio makes sure that the hundreds of restaurants that serve his bread do not run short. What he can't control is how they serve it.

"I always try to impress on a restaurant that if I give them fresh bread today and they serve it tomorrow, it's me who looks bad," says Fazio, who at the age of twenty-five took over Joe Fazio Bakery, Inc., at 1717 Sublette Avenue on the Hill. "And all my bread is delivered in paper bags. Plastic ruins the crust."

Some restaurants do right by Fazio's, which is the largest independently owned bakery in the area. One night, Fazio was heading into a favorite eatery just as a friend was leaving. The friend had two loaves of bread with him, bread he had purchased from the restaurant. "The guy apolo-

gizes to me and says he bought the bread because he loves it," recalls Fazio. "It's okay, I tell him. It's my bread."

When Vincenzo Dimare came to the United States from Italy in 1902, he opened a bread bakery in St. Louis. The business was successful. When he died in 1926, Joe Fazio, Dimare's son-in-law, took over the business and named it Joe Fazio Bakery. Fazio turned the bakery over to his son Charlie in 1961. Charlie Fazio introduced a line of Italian specialty foods, including meat sauces and ravioli, in 1983. Today, Charlie Fazio's three children, along with his grandson and several cousins, operate the wholesale bakery. Fazio's makes more than 100 different breads and serves over 750 customers, many of them restaurants. Some of Fazio's products are available at local groceries.

Other breads featured at many restaurants are made by Companion. Siblings Josh Allen and Jodi Allen Gordon own the company, which makes more than 350 different breads and pastries. Companion also operates three Café Gathering Places, with locations in Clayton (8143 Maryland Avenue), the Central West End (4651 Maryland Avenue), and Ladue (9781 Clayton Road).

"Baking is one of those professions where after two days you either love it or you run screaming from the bakery at 4 a.m.," says Allen. "I fell in love with the craft in San Francisco in the

Courtesy of Companion

Jodi Allen Gordon and Josh Allen love the baking life. Courtesy of Companion.

Since 1913, Pratzel's Bakery has made a signature sourdough rye. "We make it using the original culture that my grandfather Max borrowed from another baker," says Ronnie Pratzel, who owns the bakery with his wife, Elaine. Pratzel figures the sourdough culture is nearly one hundred years old.

"The culture used to be grown in a wooden trough, but in the 1970s, the health department decided it had to be kept in a food-safe plastic tub," says Pratzel. "We keep it refrigerated, too. The culture can live without refrigeration, but with the summers in St. Louis—well, it could go off."

One variation of the sourdough rye is Pratzel's tzizel rye, a loaf coated in corn meal. "That's the bread we get the most inquires over," says Pratzel. "We ship it all over the country." The bakery makes several other kinds of European bread, plus bagels, rolls, specialty cakes, and numerous pastries, including a chocolate-frosted chocolate cupcake. The breads are available at some local stores and delis, and all of Pratzel's products are sold in their retail store, located in Simon Kohn's Market, 10405 Old Olive Street in Creve Coeur.

early 1990s." In 1993, at the age of twenty-three, Allen opened a wholesale business here in South St. Louis. "I only knew how to make five breads, but fortunately a handful of folks took an interest in a flour-dusted kid."

Some of those folks operated groceries, and some were restaurant owners. At the time, though some restaurants served fresh bread from Fazio's or other old-school Italian bakeries, many gave little thought to the bread they placed on tables. "People started to figure out if they could get good bread at a grocery, they ought to be able to get good bread in a restaurant, and that forced the hand of the restaurants," says Allen. "That's when restaurants started coming to me."

Patrick Judd, who owns The Daily Bread at 11719 Manchester Road in Des Peres, is another "flour-dusted" fellow who owns a bakery and café. In the late 1980s, Judd bought a mixer and some used ovens at an auction, and he started baking bread. He opened his first retail location in University City in 1993, and a second in Des Peres in 1998. In 2000, Judd closed the University City location and now makes all his bread on the premises at the Des Peres location.

Pratzel's Bakery isn't just about rye bread. Courtesy of Pratzel's Bakery.

Older than Pratzel's, older than Fazio's, now gone but not forgotten—that's Freund Baking Company, famous for "Old Tyme Rye." Moritz and Jetta Freund made their way to St. Louis from Bohemia in the early 1850s. He was a baker back home, but it was Jetta who first baked rye bread in a wood-fired stove in the cellar of their house at 913 Soulard Street.

Ronnie Pratzel (in baby carriage) goes on an outing with his uncle, Herb Yonak, and his mom, Bertha Pratzel. Courtesy of Pratzel's Bakery.

In *Zion in the Valley: The Jewish Community of St. Louis, Volume 1*, Walter Ehrlich wrote that the Freunds' first customers were neighbors entranced with the aroma of the fresh-baked bread, but word quickly spread through the city and eventually throughout the country. In 1921, the Freund family bought a building at Taylor and Chouteau that could accommodate their successful business. Four generations of Freunds made bread before a large corporation bought the company in 1972.

STARCH CITY

What's the story behind the omnipresent Saint Louis Bread Company bakeries and cafés?

Today, Panera Bread Company, a bakery-café chain based in Boston, owns Saint Louis Bread, which is known as Panera elsewhere in the country. But the chain started here in 1987, when Linda and Ken Rosenthal opened up the first Saint Louis Bread Company in Kirkwood, where they sold fresh-baked loaves of sourdough bread.

ST. LOUIS'
MOST FAMOUS NAME
IN
BAKERY PRODUCTS

Freund

Independently owned and operated in St. Louis for 106 years.

FREUND BAKING CO.

The company grew quickly, developing a lively lunch trade and later establishing Saint Louis Bread Company as a great place to stop for coffee and a pastry. In October 1993, there were twenty locations when *Inc.* magazine included Saint Louis Bread on a list of the five hundred fastest-growing privately held companies in the country. A month later, the Rosenthals and their business partners announced they were selling Saint Louis Bread Company to Au Bon Pain Company for $24 million. At the time, Au Bon Pain operated cafés under that name.

In 1997, Au Bon Pain executives decided to concentrate their efforts on the Panera Bread bakery-cafés, and in May 1999, they sold all their other business units and renamed the firm. Today, there are more than twelve hundred Panera Bread bakery-cafés spread out over forty states (thirty-eight in the metropolitan area), and the company claims to bake more bread each day than any bakery-café business in the country.

Two other national bread bakery chains have a presence here. In 1999, Duane and Kay Johnson opened Breadsmith of St. Louis at 10031 Manchester Road in Glendale. Great Harvest Bread Company has two locations: Steve and Alecia Jawor own the store at 9449 Olive Boulevard in Olivette and Donna and Mike Thibodeau are at 3843 Mexico Road in St. Charles.

Maybe our deep interest in and enjoyment of bread is somehow connected to Missouri's location, in the heart of the wheat-filled plains. Historians say that is exactly why in 1910 St. Louis was able to boast that it was "the spaghetti center of America." In her book *Food in Missouri*, Madeline Matson notes that there were ten pasta factories in town at the time.

In *Immigrants on the Hill*, author Gary Ross Mormino quotes a reporter of the day, writing for *la Montagna*, a publication for and about the Hill: "St. Louis produces a million dollars worth of spaghetti, macaroni, and noodles. Over 325 skilled workers are required to make this output possible."

Giovanni Ravarino and Giuseppe Freschi, brothers-in-law who operated a sausage factory and wholesale grocery business here, founded Ravarino and Freschi Macaroni Company in 1914 because they were concerned that imports from Italy would come to a halt during World War I. Their products won numerous international prizes, and their factory was the last to close here. Borden acquired the closed plant in 1986 and today R&F pasta is manufactured and sold throughout the country by the American Italian Pasta Company, a company founded in 1988 in Excelsior Springs, Missouri.

BLACK BEAR BAKERY: POLITICS IN THE KITCHEN

Courtesy of Black Bear Bakery

Old World breads, present-day pastries, and a varied café menu, made and served with a pinch of politics, all are available at an anti-authoritarian, anti-ideological collective that takes pride in its community involvement. Black Bear Bakery, at 2639 Cherokee, has four basic goals:

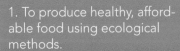

1. To produce healthy, affordable food using ecological methods.

2. To foster consensus-based decision making in a dynamic environment that challenges division-of-labor and capital-based, hierarchical business.

3. To present participants with opportunities and tools for sustenance and individual growth in a worker-controlled and operated bakery.

4. To organize and embrace anarchic grassroots agitation, information, and action.

Founded in 1998, Black Bear Bakery makes several products originally made by the Lickhalter Bakery, which opened at 1119 Biddle Street in 1915. The Lickhalters, a Russian Jewish family, specialized in rye breads (including dark pumpernickel), challah, handmade bagels, and a raisin babka. The bakery grew to be one of the largest in the city in the 1950s and 1960s.

In the 1970s, the Lickhalter family sold the bakery. In 1998, the owners left the business, and turned over the old recipes to a collective known as City of Little Bread. The name was changed to Black Bear Bakery in 1999, when it was the only bakery in town that offered two kinds of organic 100 percent whole grain breads.

"Today we make the Lickhalter breads, and we also make whole grain and multigrain breads, which are growing in popularity," says Bobby Sweet. "That's not surprising. First we got hit by the Atkins thing [a diet that prohibits the eating of bread], but people's response to that has been to eat whole grains."

The bakery also makes Vienna white bread, olive-rosemary bread, granola, and numerous pastries, including cakes, muffins, and cookies. All products are made from scratch using local, organic ingredients whenever possible.

A full-service café is new at Black Bear Bakery. Goals for the café include "making the café a very child-friendly environment, encouraging local community organizations to meet there, and accepting food stamps on all eligible sale items." Pizzas, soups, sandwiches, and breakfast items are on the menu.

Working with pasta machines imported from Italy, employees of David Burmeister's Mangia Italiano make one thousand pounds of pasta a week in a small factory in the Cherokee Street neighborhood. "We make sixteen shapes of pasta and fifteen flavors, mainly for the restaurant," says Clara Moore, pasta maker. Mangia Italiano is at 3145 South Grand. "The rest goes to wholesale. We sell pasta to fifteen or twenty restaurants in St. Louis, and we also are in Whole Foods Market and at the Tower Groves Farmers' Market. We definitely are interested in keeping this art alive."

In business since 1964, Louisa Food Products, at 1918 Switzer Avenue, manufactures and distributes frozen beef ravioli, cannelloni meat sauces, roast beef, and pasta. Maria & Son, at 4201 Hereford, specializes in ravioli and meat sauce—and a line of frozen crab rangoon and egg rolls and bottled curry sauces, as well.

Harinder Singh, who owns the India's Rasoi and Curry in a Hurry restaurants, and his business partner, John Ard, introduced the Asian foods when they bought the shuttered Maria & Son Italian Products, Inc., in 2004. Phyllis and Louis Cannovo started Maria & Son in 1961. Their grandson, Tony Cannovo, runs the plant now for Singh and Ard. "I have the first dollar my grandparents made," says Cannovo. "I keep it in a fireproof box."

Take one look at the specialty products from Gus' Pretzels, and you may consider keeping them for posterity, too. Founded in 1920 and famous for their traditional pretzel sticks, the company, at 1820 Arsenal Street, also makes heart-shaped pretzels for Valentine's Day, shamrocks for St. Patrick's Day, crosses for First Communion, pumpkins for Halloween, trees for Christmas, and a pretzel in the shape of a football in honor of the Rams. Need an alternative to a birthday cake? Gus' Pretzels will wrestle pretzel twists into numbers.

A major producer of pet food—Ralston Purina—actually got its name from producing whole grain cereal. In 1898, company founder William H. Danforth extracted the name *Purina* from the company's slogan: "Where purity is paramount." Danforth approached popular nutritionist Albert Edgerly, better known as Dr. Ralston, to endorse his cereal. The collaboration was so successful that the company name was changed to Ralston Purina Company.

Courtesy of Gus' Pretzels

Gus Koebbe, Sr., holds his daughter Karen in the kitchen at Gus' Pretzels in this photo from 1953. Courtesy of Gus' Pretzels.

BEYOND STARCH—WAY BEYOND

When it comes to food manufacturing, starting small can lead to big things. That's a philosophy embraced by the St. Louis Enterprise Centers, a partnership among the St. Louis Development Corporation, the St. Louis County Economic Council, and the St. Louis Small Business Development Partnership. The Enterprise Centers, also known as "incubators," offer small businesses office and warehouse space; office, receptionist, and warehouse services; management counseling; networking opportunities; and low-cost loans for some clients.

The Midtown Enterprise Center near downtown on Washington Avenue houses a two thousand-square-foot commercial kitchen for clients interested in producing food. Tenants at the kitchen incubator, in operation since 2005, are whipping up everything from flan to brownies to cookies. Roslyn Wicks, site administrator, notes that several local food producers got their start at the kitchen incubator, among them:

- Batter Up! Cookies
- Berhanu Organic
- The Brownie Factory
- DB Gourmet Cookies
- Dogtown Pizza
- Kakao Chocolates

The Mound City Shelled Nut Company, in business since 1917, makes fresh peanut butter. Their retail store is at 7831 Olive Boulevard in University City. George Hubbard of O'Fallon, Illinois, produces Original Gringo Salsas, made piquant from peppers grown in Hubbard's own garden. Speaking of spicy, Red Hot Riplets potato chips from Old Vienna in Fenton garnered praise in 2004 from *Esquire* magazine. Louis Kaufman founded Old Vienna Snack Food Company here in 1936. The firm transferred hands several times, and in 2006, the brand was purchased and revived by Steve Hoffman and other former employees.

Volpi Foods, which specializes in traditional Italian dry-cured meats, started out as a family business in 1902 and remains just that. Giovanni Volpi, who trained as a *salumiere* (salami maker) in Milan and brought his skills to the United States in 1900, founded the company at 5254 Daggett on the Hill. His nephew, Armando Pasetti, came here from Italy in 1938 to learn the business and to continue the tradition. On Pasetti's watch, Volpi Foods combined tradition with progressive technology and also greatly expanded product distribution.

SINETSIDK BERHANU: LOVING THOSE LENTILS

Courtesy of Nancy L. Bridges

Sinetsidk Berhanu is on a mission. "I want to convince people that healthy food is delicious," says Berhanu, a native of Ethiopia, a former restaurant owner, and grandmother of five.

To accomplish that, Berhanu has concocted Ah! Zeefa dips, made of black lentils, fresh lime, olive oil, herbs, and spices. For those who like spicy foods, one version of the dip is available with serrano peppers added, and one with jalapenos. The dips also serve as a tasty sandwich spread.

"Black beluga lentils taste a little different from other lentils," explains Berhanu. "They are on the sweet side, and they are filled with antioxidants." Berhanu started making all three varieties of the dip in July 2007 at the St. Louis Enterprise Center in midtown, where she and other budding food producers have the use of a commercial kitchen.

"My heart has always been in the food business," says Berhanu, who came to St. Louis in 1971. In the 1980s, she owned Sine Qua Non, an Ethiopian restaurant here. Later, she developed a product called Lentils Divine, which Berhanu packaged in nine flavors. The food manufacturing business "outgrew" her, she says, and she turned to teaching art in the St. Louis public schools for five years.

Then the kitchen called her back. "I love to cook, I love the kitchen, I love to create," exults Berhanu. "In the kitchen, I have the freedom to be my own slave."

Berhanu Organic, her company, currently offers the Ah! Zeefa dips, Lentils Divine, and Berhanu Breakfast, a quick-cooking blend of organic buckwheat and spices. "Flavor and health," reiterates Berhanu. "I am working to combine the two."

In 2002, Pasetti's daughter Lorenza was named president of Volpi Foods. The original factory is still in use, but the company has grown to fill two additional buildings. Today, Volpi Foods makes 75,000 pounds of salami and 90,000 pounds of prosciutto (dry-cured Italian ham) each week. The company makes fourteen different salamis, five specialty meats (including coppa and pancetta), two kinds of prosciutto, and five varieties of Rotola, a product unique to Volpi Foods that combines mozzarella cheese with prosciutto or salami. Ninety-nine percent of the business is wholesale, and Volpi products are sold all over the country and throughout much of the world. (Check out Volpi on www.amazon.com!) St. Louisans are lucky—we can just drive to Volpi's deli at 5250 Daggett.

Don't be surprised if visitors from out of town know about Volpi Foods. Celebrity chefs Mario Batali and Michael Chiarello are fans—in fact, Chiarello calls Volpi Foods "the best domestic artisan salami producer" and has produced a line of artisan salami with Volpi under his own brand, Napa Style. The Food Network featured Volpi in the *Road Tasted* series, and some of Pasetti's recipes were included in *The Deen Bros. Cookbook: Recipes from the Road.*

Salami made with Chianti or Pinot Grigio wine is a new product line from Volpi Foods. Courtesy of Volpi Foods.

LORENZA PASETTI: THE BEST OF THE OLD AND THE NEW

Courtesy of Volpi Foods

Responsibility for producing world-class salami and prosciutto—not to mention the challenge of running a successful business founded in 1902—rests on the capable shoulders of Lorenza Pasetti, president of Volpi Foods.

Every day, Pasetti balances the burden of a time-honored tradition with obvious enthusiasm for her work. "It doesn't help that everyone in my family is a food critic," she says, laughing. Pasetti remembers working side by side with her sisters when they were youngsters. "Our parents said we could go swimming when we finished wrapping salami, and I stood there wishing that no more orders would come in, so we could leave."

Pasetti also worked in the shop at 5250 Daggett, and when she was older, she handled online orders "as a hobby." Over time, Pasetti has worked in every aspect of the business. As president, she is making changes that fit with the original philosophy of the venerable business and also reflect a respect for the growing interest in natural foods.

For instance, she is reviewing plans to remove all nitrates and nitrites from Volpi products, and the company already has reverted to using a natural casing in 50 percent of the products. "Originally, there were no nitrites, no nitrates, and no collagen casings. We always had a simple ingredient list," says Pasetti. "I'm also working with family farms that raise animals for certain of our product lines."

Volpi Foods' newest product is wine salami, introduced in 2007. One is made with Pinot Grigio and one with Chianti. "The products are wrapped in butcher paper, with a label that appears to be handwritten," says Pasetti, "like Grandpa would do."

Every year in December, Pasetti works in the deli. "First, they need the help. Second, it always puts me in the Christmas mood. Third, it gives me a chance to hear what the customers are saying," she says. "Here at Volpi, it's all about the product."

Top: With his co-workers, young salumiere Armando Pasetti (at right) shows off Volpi products in a photo from 1944.

Above: Armando Pasetti is still working, and he is still proud of Volpi products. Courtesy of Volpi Foods.

WELCOME!

MAKES STEAKS SURPRISINGLY DIFFERENT!

Maull's

THE GENUINE
Barbecue Sauce

BROADWAY
AND
NORTH MARKET

Much of the salsiccia (Italian sausage) served at restaurants in town comes from Manzo Importing Company, in business since 1955. The company produces handcrafted Italian salsiccia and sells other meats, spices, olive oils, and tomato products. Manzo also operates a retail store at 5346 Devonshire where you can buy a variety of products, including four kinds of hand-crafted salsiccia: Traditional (with fennel seeds), hot, tomato (with chunks of fresh tomatoes and aged Parmesan), and extra special (with aged Parmesan, fresh tomatoes, parsley, and sweet Marsala wine).

If bratwurst is your sausage of choice, readers of *The Riverfront Times* declared in 2005 that the Best Bratwurst comes from G&W Meat & Bavarian Style Sausage Company at 4828 Parker Avenue. In business for over forty years, G&W makes their sausages from an old family recipe originally developed in Regensburg, Germany. Want sauce on that brat? St. Louis is home to a small company that makes barbecue sauce—Super Smokers, which also runs a barbecue joint in Eureka—and a big company that makes barbecue sauce—Maull's, which started in 1897 as a grocery wholesaler specializing in cheese and fish.

Another company that started with cheese in 1934 stuck with it—the Hautly Cheese Company, makers of American cheese, Ricotta, and string and stick cheeses. The company moved to Fenton in June 2008 after many years on the Hill. Provel cheese, the pizza topping of choice in our town, was never made here, though it was developed for wholesale grocer Tony Costa, who had a store downtown in the early 1960s. Abe "Toots" Pezzani at the Roma Grocery Company at 5851 Elizabeth Avenue now distributes provel for the Churny Company, a subsidiary of Kraft Foods.

Lasco Foods, Inc., at 4553 Gustine, was founded over fifty years ago as the manufacturing division of a century-old grocery and merchandise outlet. Originally one of the Allen family businesses, Lasco Foods manufactures products for the food service industry. Among the products are beverage mixes, cocktail mixes, desserts, gravy and sauce mixes, soup bases, seasonings, and salad dressings.

Arcobasso Foods, Inc., at 8014 North Broadway also knows something about salad dressings. The company makes 8,400 gallons of salad dressings, sauces, and marinades a day—and many of those dressings, sauces, and marinades are under the name of popular local restaurants.

"My brother Tom owned Drassina's, a restaurant at Big Bend and 141, where he made a thick, creamy anchovy salad dressing," recalls Pat Newsham, president of Arcobasso. "A member

The manufacturing lines are busy at Arcobasso Foods, which makes more than 8,400 gallons of salad dressings, sauces, and marinades every day. Many of the products are marketed under the names of popular local restaurants. Courtesy of Arcobasso Foods.

of the Schnuck family who ate at Drassina's liked the dressing and suggested that my brother bottle it and sell it in groceries."

Tom Newsham found a manufacturer and did just that, but eventually decided he could make the product himself. In 1987, he went into business with the Arcobasso family in a building in Baden, the same site where the company is today. The first salad dressing Arcobasso's made was for Zia's Restaurant on the Hill, and it was a hit. Fittingly, when Arcobasso responded to customer inquiries for a dressing made with artificial sweetener, Zia's was again the first.

"We try to stay ahead of the curve," says Pat Newsham, who joined the company in 1990. "Now customers are interested in fruit-flavored dressings, products with sweet heat. Our corporate chef also is looking into all-natural dressings, organic products, and products with no preservatives."

Today, Tom Newsham owns the company. The Arcobasso family is no longer involved, but Pat Newsham appreciates the serendipity of the name. In Italian, *arcobasso* means "base of the arch."

Just north of the base of the Arch, where Laclede's Landing is today, Fred M. Switzer and Joseph Murphy founded a company in 1884, producing what an advertisement from the day described as "licorice and cherry red candy packaged in bites, bars, whips and stix." In 1966, Beatrice Foods, a national food producer, bought Switzer Licorice. (Thirty years later, ConAgra bought Beatrice Foods.)

"Beatrice sold Switzer's to another firm that then sold it to Hershey, and we got it back in 2003," says Michael Switzer, a grandson of the founder. "We're making black licorice and cherry candy. We don't call the cherry candy 'licorice' because the people who eat black licorice consider that heresy." The new Switzer's products are sold in major grocery chains in several regional markets and also in the Cracker Barrel restaurants. Switzer soon plans to introduce additional licorice . . . er, candy . . . products in cherry, green apple, lemonade, cinnamon, and blue raspberry flavors.

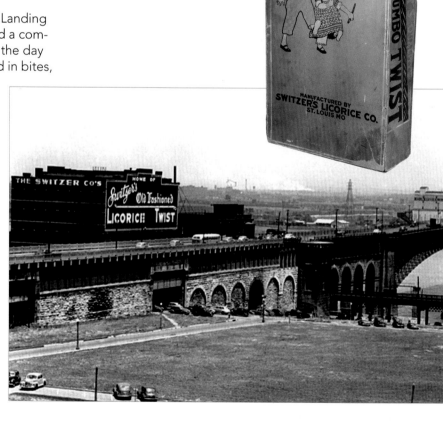

Switzer's Factory serves as a tasty backdrop for Eads Bridge in this photo taken in 1946. Courtesy of Arteaga Photos.

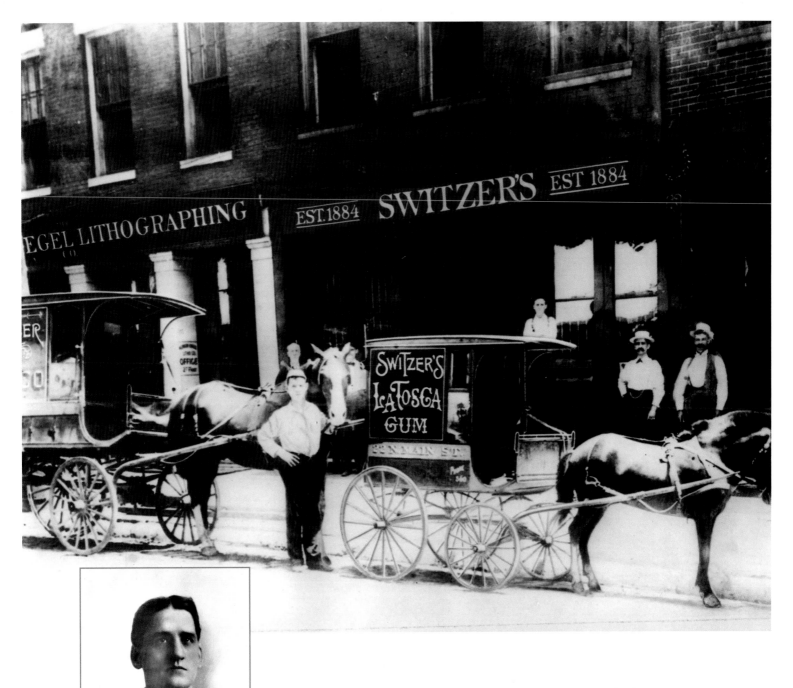

Fred M. Switzer (inset) founded his company in 1884, back in the day when food products were delivered in horse-drawn carts. Courtesy of Switzer's.

SWEET TOOTH

If your sweet tooth craves something other than licorice, you can bite into premium chocolates (milk or dark) made in St. Louis at Bissinger's Handcrafted Chocolatier (three stores), Chocolate Chocolate Chocolate (a dozen locations in the metropolitan area), Crown Candy Kitchen (1401 St. Louis Avenue), Lake Forest Confections (7801 Clayton Road), or Merb's Candies (three locations).

Bakeries have flourished here for over a century, feeding us sweet treats of every description. Although the number of bakeries remaining today pales in comparison to the 250-plus in the 1920s, quality and tradition prevail. McArthur's Bakery has been serving up wedding cakes for more than fifty years. Helen Lubeley of Lubeley's Bakery has been specializing in German pastries since she founded the bakery with her husband, Ed, in 1937. The Missouri Baking Company at 2027 Edwards was founded by Stefano Gambaro and Franco Arpiani, who did their apprenticeship at the Knickerbocker Hotel in New York and then opened a bakery in Hackensack, New Jersey, with Franco's brother Eugene.

The three men moved to St. Louis to provide bread and pastries for a restaurant owned by a relative—Ben Garavelli, who had a place on Grand Boulevard at the time. Gambaro and the Arpiani brothers opened the Missouri Baking Company on Grand and Tholozan in 1923. Two years later, they moved their business to its present location. As their retail business grew, they eventually stopped filling wholesale orders. The building has been enlarged and renovated several times, and all baking is done on the premises.

The second generation (Lino, Frank, Steve, and Ben Gambaro, along with their sister, JoAnn Gambaro Arpiani) took over the bakery in 1943. Today, siblings Mimi Gambaro Lordo and Chris Gambaro (Ben's daughter and son) own Missouri Baking Company.

The bakery makes twenty-eight different cookies all year round, including the butterball, the fig bar, and the ice box cookie. The top-selling cookie is the amaretto macaroon, says Diane Gambaro, who works at the bakery. Here is a story that proves just how good these cookies are: Two women walk into the Missouri Baking Company. One buys three cookies. One buys a five-pound box. The first woman asks, "Are you having people over?" The second woman's reply is to the point: "No."

Chocolate drops (pound cake iced in chocolate fondant) are another favorite at the Missouri Baking Company, as are the cannoli, which actually are made at Rosciglione Bakery at 2265 Bluestone Drive in St. Charles, where the bakers specialize in Italian desserts. St. Louis also is home to dozens of neighborhood bakeries, and some feature German, Korean, Mexican, Chinese, and Danish treats.

In the 1920s, Hausel's was one of about 250 bakeries in St. Louis. The bakery was at Ninth and Geyer in the Soulard neighborhood. Courtesy of Helen Lubeley.

THE CHOCOLATE WAR:
KELLERHALS AND KOLBRENER

Courtesy of Bissinger's

The Chocolate War is different from all other wars. In this war, everybody wins, especially chocoholics.

First of all, the lawsuit that Bissinger's Handcrafted Chocolatier filed against Lake Forest Confections in April 2005 for allegedly copying "trademarks, products, graphic fonts, recipes, processes and store appearance" has been settled, so now we can all get back to what really matters—enjoying celebrated handcrafted chocolates from both purveyors.

Here's the story: Ken Kellerhals (and other investors) owns Bissinger's, which has three retail shops in town, one of them inside a dessert café. Bud Kolbrener owns Lake Forest Confections at 7801 Clayton Road. Before he opened Lake Forest, Kolbrener owned Bissinger's from 1974 until 1996, when he sold the business to Kellerhals.

Bissinger's, in case you've been spending your money on Hershey's all these years, dates back to seventeenth-century Paris, where the Bissinger family first made fine chocolates to tempt the palates of everybody who was anybody—Louis XIV, Ludwig of Bavaria, and Josephine Bonaparte, for instance—in Europe. In 1845, Karl Bissinger and his master candy maker moved to the United States, settling in Ohio. Karl Bissinger's son (also named Karl) moved to St. Louis in 1927, where he opened a candy shop on McPherson Avenue in the Central West End.

In June 2007, Kellerhals closed that original shop and opened Bissinger's: A Chocolate Experience, at 32 Maryland Avenue. "It's a place to more fully experience chocolate," says Katherine Drinen, brand manager at Bissinger's. "You can experience candy there as well as sit down in the lounge and have chocolate desserts with wine, coffee, or liqueurs." The dessert café seats twenty-two people. Special events include a happy hour and a class on the third Monday of every other month where participants learn to pair five wines with five chocolates.

Courtesy of Lake Forest Confections

Bissinger's also has retail shops at the Saint Louisa Galleria, Plaza Frontenac, and in Edina, Minnesota. A mail order catalog brings Bissinger's to the rest of the country.

After Kolbrener sold Bissinger's to Kellerhals, Kolbrener retired, spending his time traveling and participating in culinary classes around the world. What propelled him back into the chocolate business?

"When I left Bissinger's, I wanted out," says Kolbrener. "I had built it up into a huge business, and I was tired of working so hard. I originally liked the business because I liked seeing people, and I liked making candy. But when you get big, you spend all your time going to meetings."

At Lake Forest Confections, Kolbrener now works side by side with six of his former employees from Bissinger's, making every chocolate confection sold in the store. "Before, I was an executive. Now, I'm making candy again, in little batches—ten pounds of this, twelve pounds of that. It's a lot more fun."

Top: Helen Lubeley (middle right) serves customers at the bakery that she and her husband, Ed, opened in 1937.

Above: Ed, Jr. (left) works in the family business today. Located at 7815 Watson Road, Lubeley's Bakery and Deli specializes in German pastries and cookies. Courtesy of Lubeley's Bakery.

Newcomers include two bakeries specializing in cupcakes: The Cupcakery at 28 Maryland Plaza in the Central West End and Jilly's Cupcake Bar at 8509 Delmar in University City. *Sex in the City* may have popularized gourmet cupcakes, but Tim Brennan says he created a cupcake wedding cake fifteen years ago for a customer who clearly was ahead of the curve.

Brennan, who owns Cravings Gourmet Desserts and Café at 8149 Big Bend Boulevard in Webster Groves, started crafting confections, including wedding cakes, in 1984 in a church kitchen in the Soulard neighborhood. His retail business steadily grew, and in 1993, he opened Cravings. Here is a partial list of ingredients Brennan uses in one year:

- One ton of butter
- Two tons of chocolate
- Five thousand eggs
- Two thousand cups of cream
- Ten thousand pounds of sugar

Two of Brennan's desserts have been honored with James Beard Awards, and in December 2006, Cravings was listed in *USA Today*'s article on "Ten Great Places to Indulge Your Sweet Tooth."

Hank Krussel of Hank's Cheesecakes has been turning out his specialty cheesecakes since 1983, first as a caterer and, after 1984, from his bakery, now located at 1063 South Big Bend in Richmond Heights. Krussel learned to bake cheesecake while in the Army, and he's never looked back.

Hank's cheesecakes have won much national recognition, and so has the artist whose work graces the box in which each sweet or savory cheesecake from Hank's is packed. Mary Grand Pre, a former St. Louisan, is the artist, and she also illustrated the American versions of J. K. Rowling's Harry Potter novels.

THE OFFICIAL STATE DESSERT

On May 14, 2008, the Missouri legislature declared the ice cream cone the Official State Dessert. How did that happen?

Nineteen youngsters in the St. Louis area are responsible for the designation. The students, part of a home-school cooperative, are Annamarie (Elise) Kostial; Alexandra D'Ordine; Kjia Zuroweste; Garrett and Elise Floyd; Jacob, Nicholas, and Bethany Frost; Grace Savage; Louisa Geyer; Elizabeth and Katie Kramer; Thatcher Broyles; Kayleigh Hecht; Anna, Nathan, and Gabriel Farrell; and Chloe and Josie Lozano. They ranged in age from eight to thirteen.

According to their website (www.themissouriicecreamcone.org), the students hoped this designation "would provide an additional marketing tool for Missouri ice cream and dairy companies." They did their homework before approaching the legislature. The students learned that St. Louis is the fourth largest city in ice cream consumption, that Missouri ranks tenth in ice cream production, and that this is the fifth largest dairy state.

They already knew that the ice cream cone was developed at the 1904 World's Fair. They lined up industry sponsors and then convinced Senator John Loudon and Representative Charlie Schlottach to sponsor the bill. The students' hard work paid off. Effective August 28, 2008, Missouri had an Official State Dessert.

The Ted Drewes Frozen Custard stand at 6726 Chippewa opened in 1941, ten years after the stand at 4224 South Grand. The original location in St. Louis opened in 1930 on Natural Bridge Avenue.

In St. Louis, you can fill your cone with ice cream, gelato, sorbet, frozen yogurt, or frozen custard. Serendipity Homemade Ice Cream at 8130 Big Bend Boulevard in Webster Groves adds and changes flavors often, but among the possibilities are coffee almond, chocolate chip, caramel apple, cake batter, dulce de leche, English toffee, butter pecan, and Vermont maple walnut. The Karandzieff family has been making ice cream at Crown Candy Kitchen since they opened in 1913 at 1401 St. Louis Avenue.

Here's the scoop on Quezel Sorbets and Glaces: After hanging his political science degree on the wall and working in various aspects of food service, Ron Ryan went to Paris where a French chef taught him to make sorbet. On July 20, 1979, he opened his own business back home in St. Louis. He started with one flavor—raspberry, made from fresh fruit at the peak of ripeness. Today, Ryan makes half a dozen flavors of sorbet, plus premium ice creams, and he sells them to restaurants and at some groceries. Ryan also created Ronnie's Rocky Mountain, a dark-chocolate-topped ice cream treat sold every summer at the Muny and the Saint Louis Zoo.

Gelato di Riso scoops up creamy Italian ice cream at 9905 Manchester Road in Warson Woods and also uses gelato in pies and cakes. Among the gelato flavors available are amaretto, hazelnut, strawberry, raspberry, blackberry, pistachio, and tiramisu. Frozen custard stands nestle in many a neighborhood, but Ted Drewes, here since 1930, is the best known. The custard stand at 4224 South Grand is open only during the summer, but the Ted Drewes at 6726 Chippewa closes only in January.

Pevely Dairy uses the mystique of the 1904 World's Fair to sell their ice cream. They earned the right: Pevely provided all the milk to the Fair. Pevely founder Casper Kerckhoff named his company after the town just south of St. Louis. Kerckhoff emmigrated from Germany in the early 1840s, and two of his many, many children—twenty-three in all—relocated to Seventh Street in downtown St. Louis. Presently located on sixteen acres at the corner of Grand and Chouteau, Pevely is now a subsidiary of Prairie Farms, which purchased the dairy in 1989. Prairie Farms is a major Midwest dairy cooperative that was founded in 1932 and is based in Illinois.

Facing: A family at the 1904 World's Fair tries out a new-fangled treat. Courtesy of Missouri History Museum, St. Louis.

Left: Prairie Farms ice cream is a common sight in St. Louis grocery stores and refrigerators. Courtesy Mid-America Grocers Association.

Need something to clear your palate after all that ice cream? Just Whistle.

Whistle, of course, is the popular orange-flavored soft drink produced by Vess Soda, founded here in 1916. Charles Leiper Grigg, a Vess employee, developed Whistle. "The Billion Bubble Beverage" comes in other flavors too, among them cola, cream, lemon-lime, pineapple, blueberry, and kiwi-strawberry. Today, the Vess brand is owned by Cott Corporation, one of the world's largest non-alcoholic beverage companies and the world's largest retailer-brand soft drink provider.

In 1953, the Vess Bottling Company commissioned a sign company to build a giant revolving soda bottle lit with neon tubing. Thirty-five-and-a-half feet tall, the Vess Soda Bottle originally was erected at Hampton Avenue and Gravois Boulevard, where it revolved on a steel pole for decades. At some point, the bottle was dismantled and placed in storage. In 1989, it was re-erected on a stationary pole at 520 O'Fallon Street near Sixth Street, west of Laclede's Landing.

The man who developed Whistle also devised the recipe for 7-UP. In 1920, Charles Leiper Grigg left Vess and founded his own soft drink company, the Howdy Corporation. In 1929, Grigg concocted a caramel-colored formula for a lemon-lime soft drink, which he named "Bib-Label Lithiated Lemon-Lime Soda."

Catchy, huh?

Lithium citrate—a mood stabilizer—was one of the ingredients, and the beverage was marketed as a medicinal product useful for curing hangovers. At the time, there were some six hundred lemon-lime beverages in the market. After a well-advised name change, 7-UP flourished, and by the late 1940s, the beverage had become the third best-selling soft drink in the world. Happy with the success of his nationally distributed product, in 1936 Grigg renamed his firm the Seven Up Company.

(Forget about using 7-UP to boost your mood—in 1950, lithium citrate was removed from the formula.)

In 1967, the Seven-Up Company started marketing its signature beverage as the Uncola, a moniker that stuck through several advertising campaigns. Philip Morris acquired the company in 1978. Eight years later, 7-UP's domestic operations were purchased by a private investment group that later merged with the Dr Pepper Company, which is based in Dallas. Cadbury Schweppes bought Dr Pepper /Seven-Up Companies in 1995.

Courtesy of Matthew Heidenry

Orange and lemon-lime soft drinks have their place in any line of soft drinks, of course, but root beer is a beverage of a different color—literally and historically. Root beer originated in colonial America, when individuals brewed their own beverages. A typical root beer recipe of the day called for a gallon and a half of molasses, five gallons of boiling water, one-fourth pound each of sarsaparilla root, bruised sassafras bark, and birch bark, one-half pint of fresh yeast, and enough additional water to make sixteen gallons.

Charles Hires, a pharmacist in Philadelphia, claimed to have developed a particularly tasty recipe that called for more than twenty-five herbs, berries, and roots added to carbonated soda water. Hires introduced his beverage to the public at the 1876 Philadelphia Centennial Exposition, the first official world's fair held in the United States. Today, root beer is said to account for less than 3 percent of the soda market, so it's especially interesting that two root beers originated in St. Louis: IBC and Fitz's.

IBC dates back to 1919, when the savory beverage was produced by the Independent Breweries Company, a firm comprised of nine local breweries that pooled resources in 1907. The idea at the time was that the merger would give small brewers a realistic shot at competing with Anheuser-Busch and the St. Louis Brewing Association. It didn't. Only IBC Root Beer, originally produced during Prohibition, survived.

When the Independent Breweries Company closed, the Kranzberg family purchased the root beer brand and distributed the beverage from their Northwestern Bottling Company here. The Kranzbergs sold the IBC trademark and the formula in the late 1930s to the National Bottling Company, but after a good run in the 1930s and 1940s, IBC Root Beer declined in popularity. Taylor Beverages bought the brand in 1976. Four years later, Taylor sold the brand to the Seven-Up Company. When the Dr Pepper Company bought the Seven-Up Company in 1976, IBC Root Beer was part of the deal. Today, as part of Cadbury Schweppes, the IBC soft drink line includes black cherry, cherry, and cream sodas in addition to the root beer.

Nostalgia for a specific brand of root beer led to the lively eatery now known as Fitz's American Grill & Bottling Works at 6605 Delmar in University City. The precursor was a drive-in near the intersection of Clayton Road and Brentwood Boulevard in

Richmond Heights. In 1946, James Fitzpatrick bought an old A&W Root Beer stand, named his place Fitz's, and started making homemade root beer.

Much to the dismay of area teenagers who liked to gather at Fitz's, the owner retired in the early 1970s and the place closed. Fast-forward to 1985. Tom Cohen, a local architect, was out jogging with a friend in the flavor business. On this hot, muggy day, Cohen suddenly had a yen for a frosty Fitz's Root Beer, his beverage of choice when he was a child. Mostly in jest, he suggested to his friend that they find the original formula and make the root beer.

Wise in the ways of the soft drink business, Cohen's friend discouraged him from pursuing the fantasy. Cohen didn't listen. He found the formula, registered the name, and started cooking root beer in his kitchen, working to blend the perfect flavor. Three years later, Fitz's Root Beer was available in thirty-five local specialty shops, small groceries, and restaurants.

Just about the time Fitz's Restaurant opened in the Loop, Cohen went back to architecture. The restaurant changed hands several times, and today Fitz's is owned by Clayton Capital Partners, a private investment group. Fans of Fitz's Root Beer, old and new, gather at Fitz's American Grill & Bottling Works for a cold frosty mug and to watch the bottling line, which can turn out a bottle of Fitz's Root Beer (or cream soda or orange soda) every second.

At Carl's Drive-In in Brentwood, the root beer is homemade, cooked up every six or seven days, drawn from oak barrels, and served in frosty mugs.

Raise a glass of root beer—or your beverage of choice—to all the entrepreneurs producing food and beverages here, and all those to come.

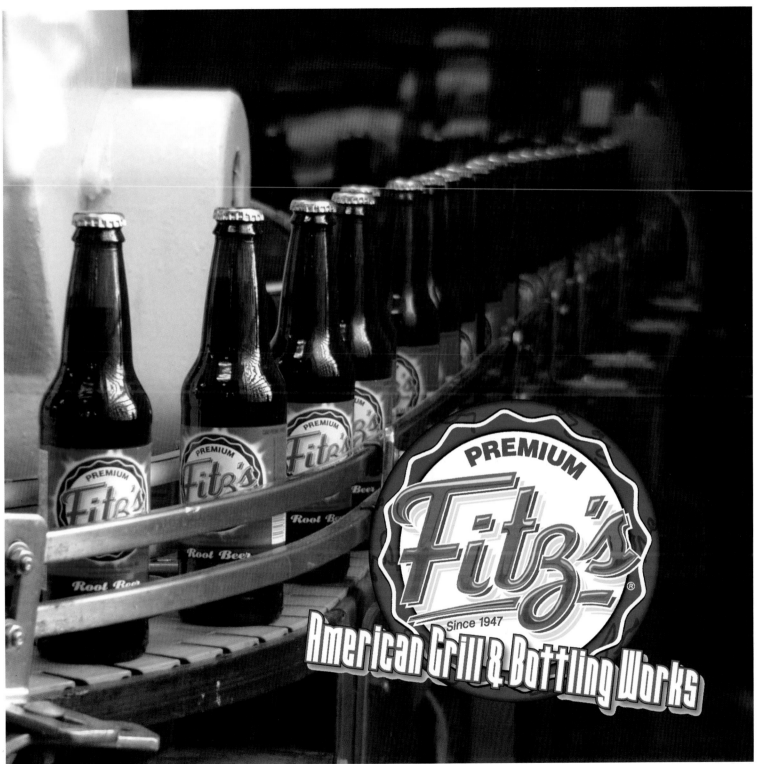

Courtesy of Fitz's

Chapter 3

TO MARKET,
TO MARKET:
GROCERIES

In 1885, a 2,300-pound wheel of cheese lured customers to A. Moll Grocery Company at 614 Franklin Avenue. Manufactured for Moll's by three factories in Sheboygan, Wisconsin, the cheese measured six feet in diameter and three feet thick. Customers who came in to gawk also placed orders—and within three weeks, Moll's had sold more than a ton of the cheese.

Above: Moll's Grocery had been feeding St. Louisans for almost fifty years when this photo was taken in 1900. Courtesy of the Library of Congress.

Previous Page: Before Produce Row was established north of downtown in 1953, vendors sold fresh produce from storefronts and stalls along Third Street. Courtesy of Clarence Hughes.

Dan Shaul, director of the Mid-America Grocers Association, laughs when he hears this story. "Have we really changed much? Groceries today still provide stuff from all over and offer gimmicks to get you into the store."

Shaul turns serious. "In some ways, the grocery industry is the fabric of a city. Walk into a grocery in any neighborhood in any city, look at what is on the shelves and in the refrigerator cases and you can learn about the people who live there."

Shaul knows groceries. The Mid-America Grocers Association, based in St. Louis, represents about 700 members in eastern Missouri and southern Illinois. Shaul also is director of the larger Missouri Grocers Association, a nonprofit organization that represents more than 1,300 members of the grocery industry in Missouri. Retailers, wholesalers, distributors, brokers, suppliers, vendors, and manufacturers all are part of that industry, which employs about 60,000 individuals and generates nearly $10 billion in annualized retail sales.

Missouri has long been a player in the food business. In January 1852, the St. Louis Chamber of Commerce issued a report on trade, commerce, and manufacturers here that states, "In Liverpool and London, the character of St. Louis provisions stands deservedly higher than those from any other city in the west."

The report calculates that $3.5 million in provisions passed through St. Louis each year at the time, and that the grocery trade, next to the produce business, was "the most important branch of trade." Then, a bit of interstate backbiting: "St. Louis has for many years been a large distributor of groceries to the inferior and adjoining states."

In 1841, twenty wholesale groceries were in business in St. Louis, bringing in a total of $1.5 million a year. Four years later, the total income had increased by 100 percent. By 1920, groceries and grocery sundries ranked third in city businesses.

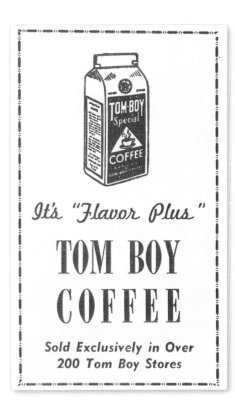

It's "Flavor Plus"

TOM BOY COFFEE

Sold Exclusively in Over 200 Tom Boy Stores

A Mid-America Grocers Association convention in days gone by drew Roger Dierberg (left), Clarence Shaul, and Bob Snyder, Sr. Courtesy of Mid-America Grocers Association.

A year later, the St. Louis Chamber of Commerce boasted there were thirty "wholesale grocery houses" in town, handling "canned pineapple from Hawaii, sugar from Cuba, olives from Spain, tea and spices from the Far East, fish from canneries on either coast, cheese from Switzerland, and currants from Greece." In the spirit of local pride, the chamber's bulletin refers to St. Louis as "the city surrounded by the United States."

Back to Shaul's original question: Have grocery stores changed much?

Yes. And no.

In the old days, there were fewer items in stores, and food prices were lower. In 1908, salt cost one dollar a barrel, sugar was just over five cents a pound, and coffee was ten cents a pound. Also, people used to shop every day—they had to, because of lack of refrigeration—and they routinely went to more than one store.

As a girl, a St. Louis woman now in her eighties recalls accompanying her mother on shopping trips in the 1930s. "First, we would go to the Mount Auburn Market in Wellston, where farmers brought in food from the country," she says. "In those days, of course, Florissant was considered the country. Next, we would head to the butcher, the bakery, the poultry store—and then we would stop at Lewis Fruit Store, which sold only fruit. I remember my mother buying cherries for ten cents a pound."

Today, you won't find cherries for ten cents a pound, no matter how much time you spend comparison shopping. However, you will find about 45,000 items for sale—and that includes nine different kinds of Cheerios. The Food Marketing Institute, a trade association based in Arlington, Virginia, reports that the typical consumer now makes 1.9 trips to a supermarket each week, and each visit results in a tab of about twenty-nine dollars.

Where do St. Louisans spend their grocery money? We have the big-box superstores, we have Trader Joe's, we have Whole Foods. National grocery chains dominate the market in most cities, but in St. Louis the grocery chains most familiar to us were started by local families and then built over the years, link by link. Here are their stories:

STRAUB'S MARKETS

Straub's Markets, the smallest of the locally owned chains, is the oldest. William A. Straub opened the first Straub's store in Webster Groves in October 1901.

As his great grandson, J. W. "Trip" Straub, III, tells it, William Straub "would go out in his horse and buggy, get orders, ride back to the store, fill the orders and then deliver them." Straub, vice president of the family company, adds, "He stocked the staples, but he focused on the meat department, selling only the highest quality beef. We still do that today."

In 1926, Straub's moved to a larger building in Webster Groves and expanded its offerings. Over time, the store became known for stocking items requested by customers. For instance, in the 1920s, Straub's carried chocolate-covered grasshoppers and ants.

Those novelty items are no longer popular, but Straub notes that the chain still strives to please the most discerning of customers. "That's the reputation we have, and though our stores are teeny, our job has always been to fine-tune the selection of items we carry, striking a balance between the national brand products everybody wants and specialty items," he says.

In 1960, Straub's in Webster Groves moved a third time, to its current location at 211 West Lockwood. Thirteen years later, Clayton got a Straub's, which today is at 8282 Forsyth Boulevard. The Central West End location opened in 1948, at 302 North Kingshighway Boulevard. And in 1966, Straub's opened a store in Town and Country, at 13414 Clayton Road.

Forty-two years later, in 2008, Straub's opened a fifth store on the northeast corner of Clarkson and Clayton Roads in Ellisville. The 40,000-square-foot store is over three times the size of the other Straub's Markets and features a 150-seat indoor/outdoor café and a cooking school. There's more—

Facing: Grocery employees stand ready to fill orders at the Straub's store in Webster Groves in this photo taken in 1926. William Straub (inset) opened his first store in 1901. Courtesy of Straub's.

William Straub

gelato is made on the premises.

"We benefit from the more upscale clientele, customers who are well traveled, who read the food magazines and watch the Food Network," say Straub. He notes that he is proud that his stores offer those customers USDA prime steaks, fine wines, artisan cheeses, gourmet condiments, homemade chicken salad, and more than twenty different kinds of root beer available at all five stores.

Straub also is pleased that two iconic St. Louisans work part-time in his deli department: Jack Carl, longtime owner of 2 Cents Plain and Ron Protzel, longtime owner of Protzel's Delicatessen. Carl works at the Central West End store and Protzel is behind the counter in Clayton. "They are doing what they love to do, waiting on customers and working with quality merchandise," says Straub.

Twice, the National Association for the Specialty Food Trade has honored Straub's Markets as Retailer of the Year, and the chain has also been lauded as one of the Top Ten Best Places to Buy Gourmet Food Online.

"Now, with our new store in Ellisville," says Straub, "we're setting the bar even higher."

Top: Delivery trucks line up at Straub's in Clayton, ready to hit the streets with orders, in this photo taken in 1933. Courtesy of Straub's.

Above: Three generations of Straub family members (from left to right) are Jack W. Straub, Sr., J. W. "Trip" Straub, III, and Jack W. Straub. Courtesy of Straub's.

SCHNUCKS MARKETS

With more than one hundred stores, Schnucks is the largest family-owned chain based in St. Louis. That's certainly to their credit, but what many St. Louisans like best about Schnucks is that the grocery invented the pork steak.

In the late 1950s, backyard barbecues were gaining in popularity. Don and Ed Schnuck, who with their parents founded the grocery, wanted to come up with an inexpensive cut of meat to cook on the grill. They started with a pork shoulder (also called a Boston Butt), meat that typically was used for roasts and sausage. They cut the meat one-half inch thick, liked how it cooked up on a grill, and—voila!—the pork steak was born.

Go to Boston (or any other city) and talk about pork steaks, and neither the general populace nor the butchers will know whereof you speak. Invite people over for barbecue in this town and serve only ribs and brats, and someone in the crowd will complain about what's missing.

Sixty-four of Schnucks' stores are in the metropolitan area, and another thirty-nine are located elsewhere in Missouri (Cape Girardeau, Columbia, Festus, Jefferson City, Washington, Wentzville) and in Illinois, Indiana, Wisconsin, Tennessee, Mississippi, and Iowa. (In Rockford, Illinois, and in Wisconsin, the stores are known as Logli Supermarkets.)

How did "The Friendliest Stores in Town" get started?

With one small store, of course. In 1937, Edwin Schnuck started a wholesale meat business. Two years later, along with his wife, Anna, and their sons, Donald and Edward, Schnuck opened a grocery in north St. Louis, making the most of all one thousand square feet in the building. In 1946, the family opened a store more than twice that big. Just six years later, Schnuck Markets, Inc., opened its first major supermarket in Brentwood.

Many more stores followed, and in 1970, Schnucks acquired Bettendorf-Rapp, a division of Allied Foods. The acquisition more than doubled the company's size. By 1985, Schnucks was expanding outside the metropolitan area. Ten years later, Schnucks acquired the assets of the National Tea Company grocery stores, a subsidiary of Loblaw Companies Limited in Canada.

In February 2006, *Progressive Grocer*, a national monthly trade publication, named Schnucks "Outstanding Regional Independent Retailer." In February 2008, downtown dwellers learned that Scott C. Schnuck (son of Donald and currently the chairman and chief executive officer) plans to build a "loft" grocery on the lower level of the Ninth Street Garage, at the corner of Ninth and Olive.

BILL KEAGGY: MAKING A LIST

The *New York Times* called Bill Keaggy's collection "compulsive reading."

What does Keaggy collect?

Grocery lists—grocery lists abandoned in carts or found wafting about on the winds of chance in grocery store parking lots.

A designer and photographer, Keaggy, who lives in St. Louis, has almost 4,000 scrawled grocery lists. Some of the lists are on his website (www.grocerylists.org) and some, complete with commentary from Keaggy, are featured in his book, *Milk Eggs Vodka: Grocery Lists Lost and Found.*

Here, Keaggy explains his unusual hobby.

Q. What appeals to you about abandoned grocery lists?

A. Most people consider grocery lists private, yet some people leave them in carts. In 1997, I found one in a Schnucks' parking lot. I picked it up. It seemed interesting, so I decided to keep them every time I came across one.

Q. Why do you consider the lists meaningful?

A. A grocery list is ephemera. It's not supposed to be important, but these lists present a more realistic picture of people's lives than posed family portraits or the important documents that people save and cherish. And if you look at enough lists, they are just funny.

The newest Schnucks is to include a fresh food market featuring natural and organic foods, a pharmacy, a floral shop, a Kaldi's Coffee Bar, meat and seafood departments, and several prepared food stations including:

- a salad bar
- an Asian hot food bar
- a barbecue bar
- a pizza station
- a chef's grill
- a made-to-order sandwich shop
- a wine department
- a tapas tasting area

The store is expected to open in late 2008 or early 2009.

Top: In 1970, Schnucks acquired the Bettendorf-Rapp stores, including the one shown here in Hampton Village at Hampton and Chippewa.

Above: The third generation of the Schnuck family, shown here in 2007, now leads the company. From left are Mark, Todd, Nancy Schnuck Diemer, Craig, Terry, and Scott. Courtesy of Schnucks.

Facing: Schnucks' first attempt at a "bigger" retail enterprise was this 2,700-square-foot store at 4356 Manchester Avenue, which opened in 1946. Courtesy of Schnucks.

DIERBERGS

The third popular local chain has been tended to and developed by four generations of the Dierberg family. In 1914, William Dierberg bought a general store at Olive Street Road just east of where Highway 270 is today. In 1929, his sons, Bill and Fred, took over the business, and one year later, they moved Dierbergs to a new 3,500-square-foot building farther east on Olive. In 1960, the store moved once again, to its current location at the corner of Craig and Olive in Creve Coeur.

Seven years later, Bill's son Bob opened the Four Seasons store near Olive and Highway 141, four miles west of the Creve Coeur store. That store was applauded for its modern design by *Progressive Grocer.* Other Dierberg family members joined the company, and the business continued to grow. Today, there are twenty stores in the metropolitan area and two in Illinois—one in Edwardsville and one in Shiloh.

Dierbergs was the first grocery in town to offer a cooking school—quite possibly the first in the country. "It was Bob Dierberg's idea, and we believe we were the first supermarket in the United States to provide in-store cooking schools staffed by full-time professional home economists," says Barb Ridenhour, director of Consumer Affairs.

"Bob's philosophy is that good cooking starts in the supermarket where you are buying groceries," she adds. "The cooking classes introduce people to new products, show them how to use familiar products in new ways, and help keep people interested in the health aspects of food."

The classes started in 1978, at just one store, but today the Dierbergs School of Cooking operates at five locations. Recent classes include "A Chef's

Facing: Joe Vehlewald (left) and Bud Beckerle, two of Schnucks' early meat cutters, wait on customers. Courtesy of Schnucks.

Below: In 1930, Dierbergs moved into a new 3,500-square-foot building on Olive Street Road in Creve Coeur. Courtesy of Dierbergs.

World of Pasta," "Treasures from the Southwest," and "Updated Classic Desserts." Ridenhour says the classes draw more than 20,000 people each year.

"Some of our most popular sessions are the 'Couples Cook' classes, 'Girls' Night Out,' classes conducted by local restaurant chefs, and our classes for parents and children," says Ridenhour. "The cooks coming to us now are more recreational, people who enjoy the creativity of the recipes. And some come because they enjoy participating in the class as a social event."

Ridenhour has a full-time staff of nine and relies on numerous part-time workers who serve as kitchen assistants, teach classes, present in-store demonstrations, test recipes, and answer customers' questions about cooking or entertaining. Her department also is responsible for *Everybody Cooks* (the store magazine), the television show of the same name, and the cookbooks published by Dierbergs.

"The grocery retailer has become an educator for a healthy way of life," says Shaul, the director of the Mid-America Grocers Association. "Nutritional information is available throughout the stores, healthy prepared meals are available—and it's now fashionable to go down the health food aisle and see what's there. And what's there is good food!"

Shaul reports that at a national grocery convention held early in 2008, the emphasis was on sustainability and the green movement. "In the next year to eighteen months, you're going to see more of an effort in stores to be more environmentally friendly," he says. "All the retailers are interested in doing the right thing. After all, the way to stay in business is to stay connected to the consumer."

Top left: Dierbergs Markets traces its roots to a country store founded in 1854 on Olive Boulevard in Creve Coeur. Courtesy of Dierbergs.

Top right: Participants in the Couples Cook class prepare recipes provided by the staff of the Dierbergs School of Cooking. Courtesy of Tim Parker.

Above: Barb Ridenhour, Director of Consumer Services at Dierbergs. Courtesy of Steve Adams.

STARTING SMALL: LOCAL HARVEST GROCERY

In January 2006, Maddie Earnest read an article in the *New York Times* about a small chain of grocery stores in Portland, Oregon, that specializes in produce and meat supplied by local farmers. Earnest showed the article to her husband, Jason McClelland, and then emailed her friends Patrick Horine and Jenny Ryan.

"I wrote, 'Let's do it—let's open a store like this,'" recalls Earnest. "Pat wrote back to say he'd already been thinking about it." Eighteen months later, in June 2007, the two couples opened Local Harvest Grocery at 3148 Morganford Road.

Their mission for the store is twofold: To provide a place for people to purchase locally grown and produced food products and to support local farmers who grow food without pesticides and raise meat in a sustainable way. "About 20 percent of the items at the store in Portland are locally grown or produced," says Earnest. "We're aiming for 50 percent."

Some of the local food products and producers represented at Local Harvest Grocery include:

Courtesy of Local Harvest

Ah! Zeefa Lentil Spreads	Companion Baking Company	La Casita Salsas
Armando's Flan	Dogtown Pizza	Moon Day Soul Baked Goods
Berger Bluff Farm	Farrar Out Farm	Our Garden
Biver Farms	Four Seasons Baked Goods	Ozark Forest Mushrooms
Black Bear Bakery	Gelato di Riso	Prairie Grass Farms Lamb
Blue Heron Orchard	Goatsbeard Cheese	Serendipity Ice Cream
Bowood Bison	Gringo Salsa	Seven Thunder Bison
Café Glace	Heartland Dairy	Sunflower Savannah
Centennial Farms	Higher Calling Farm	Terrapin Ridge
Claverach	Kakao Chocolates	Volpi

Maddie Earnest

In addition to stocking their eight hundred-square-foot store with locally grown food and assorted environmentally friendly products, Earnest and Horine operate a deli and catering service. Originally, those operations shared space with the grocery, but in Spring 2008, they moved the deli and catering service across the street. Eventually, they hope to open a big commercial kitchen in the new space, where vendors could make their own products in the off hours.

"Moving the deli gives us more space in the store for grocery items," says Earnest. "We plan to increase the produce space, bring in specialty cheeses—and we hope to have beer and wine."

Earnest comes to this job with a master's degree in social work, though in recent years she had moved on from clinical work to fundraising. "I've always been interested in where food comes from," she explains. "I grew up in Arkansas, and I'm a gardener. Also, my dad lived on a farm."

Horine and his wife started the Tower Grove Farmers' Market in 2006. "Also, I come from a grocery store background. My dad and grandpa own groceries in southern Missouri. That's the pertinent background," he says. And the impertinent? Horine grins. "I'm a graphic designer."

Earnest has the last word: "The best thing for us is the community response. People are supportive and excited about the store—and it's nice to bring this to the city."

Courtesy of Local Harvest

Tessa Greenspan

Colorful displays of fresh fruit attract shoppers at Sappington Farmers' Market at 8400 Watson Road.
Courtesy Sappington Farmers' Market.

THE INDEPENDENT GROCER

Small, independent groceries—sometimes known as mom-and-pop stores—know all about staying connected. The secret of those that are successful is finding out what the consumer wants and providing it.

What do some consumers want?

A butcher, cutting meat to order.

Joe Herrell does exactly that at Herrell's Bestway Market in Imperial. "We've been here forty-three years, and it's because we've got fresh meat, no self service or packaged stuff," says Herrell. "That and personal service. That's how I see it."

Herrell's building dates back to the early 1900s, and it's always been a store. "First it was a general store that sold clothing, plumbing, and food," says Herrell. "There was only a small fresh meat business back then, because most farmers did their own." Herrell's brother Gene bought the store in 1964, and Joe joined him in the business soon after. Gene retired recently, but Joe still puts in sixty to eighty hours a week.

Herrell knows his customers, and he knows what they like. "They come in and pick out what they want, and I cut it fresh," he says. "Our steaks are very good, and our ground beef is fresh. I grind meat several times a day."

Fresh fruit and produce have long been the specialties of the house at Sappington Farmers' Market, an independent grocery located at 8400 Watson Road in Marlborough. Tessa Greenspan signed on in 1981 to help resurrect the fading business, and when her partners wanted out in 1995, Greenspan decided to stay. She moved the market from its original location at 11520 Gravois Road and turned the store into a multimillion-dollar business.

In January 2008, Greenspan sold the market to the Missouri Farmers Union, a cooperative in Jefferson City founded by family farmers. All parties involved say the 24,000-square-foot store will continue to feature farm-fresh produce (as well as more than two hundred kinds of cheese), with a renewed emphasis on Missouri products in other areas of the store as well. Randy Wood, a farmer from Licking, Missouri, is the new business manager.

Now that the business transaction is complete, Greenspan is not picking up her expertise and going home. She says she plans to continue to play a role at the Sappington Farmers' Market.

Greenspan has come a long way from running a produce stand in the 1970s. In 2007, the Women Grocers of America, a national trade organization out of Arlington, Virginia, named her Woman of the Year. In 2002, she was honored with the Person of the Year Award during Small Business Week in St. Louis. In the previous decade, Greenspan picked up another half dozen national, regional, and local awards saluting her for her business acumen, her generosity, and her community spirit.

Courtesy of Global Foods

Gipfel's, Tom-Boy, and IGA stores all once fed St. Louisans.
Courtesy of Mid-America Grocers Association.

Some independent groceries in town have taken the international approach. Jay International Food Company at 3172 South Grand and Global Foods at 421 North Kirkwood Road in Kirkwood both specialize in foods from around the world. Chinese water spinach, dried mudfish, wasabi paste, chihuahua cheese, Thai eggplant, chicken bologna, Brazilian fruits, Danish potato chips, and much more fill the shelves of these two stores, where few cultural favorites are overlooked.

In 1975, Thai brothers Jay and Suchin Prapaisilp opened a small grocery specializing in Asian food at South Grand and Humphrey in 1975. A dozen years later, they moved their store to its current location and expanded their focus to international foods. Noy Liam, Jay Prapaisilp's brother-in-law, now runs Jay International Food Company. (Jay has returned to Thailand.) In 2006, the store was honored with a Neighborhood Business of the Year Award. Suchin and his wife, Sue, operate Global Foods Market, which they opened in 1998. Their store won a Readers' Choice Award in 2007 from *Sauce Magazine*.

Other specialty groceries abound. J. Viviano & Sons, Inc., at 5139 Shaw on the Hill is an "old-world" Italian grocery, in business since 1949. Just a few blocks away at 5200 Daggett, DiGregorio's Italian Foods manufactures and sells food to the public and to local restaurants. LeGrand's, at 4414 Donovan, resurrected an old Tom-Boy grocery in St. Louis Hills and supplements its popular meat counter by serving an overwhelming selection of deli sandwiches to a hungry lunch crowd. World-wide International Foods, at 8430 Olive, specializes in African foods in an area otherwise known for its numerous Asian groceries. Cherokee Street offers a handful of Hispanic carnicerias, and La Tropicana Market and Café at 5001 Lindenwood has specialized in Hispanic foods since 1975. The metropolitan area also is home to groceries that cater to aficionados of Greek, Indian, Vietnamese, and Middle Eastern foods.

SAVE-A-LOT AND SHOP 'N SAVE

St. Louisans also shop at national chains, and two of them—Save-a-Lot Stores and Shop 'n Save—got their start

right here. Both now are subsidiaries of SUPERVALU, Inc., which is based in Minneapolis. The company is the third-largest grocery retailing company in the United States, boasting a national network of about 2,500 retail stores.

In the 1960s, the small family-owned groceries in the St. Louis area controlled a slightly larger share of the area's food dollars than the national chains that were here at the time: A&P, Kroger, and National. A decade later, those chains started building supermarkets.

In Nancy Hayden Hobson's book *The Save-a-Lot Story*, founder Bill Moran recounts the advantages the supermarkets had over small groceries, noting that they were brightly lit, had self-service aisles, were open longer hours, and offered more efficient check-out services.

At the time, Moran was vice president of Tom-Boy stores here, and he describes that once-popular chain as "waning" in the shadow of the spiffed-up competition. Moran had an idea for a discount grocery store. He visited a few in other cities, and then opened one in Litchfield, Illinois. The store failed. Moran didn't give up. In 1977, he opened another discount grocery in Cahokia, Illinois—the first Save-a-Lot store.

Here's what happened next: In 1978, General Grocer Company bought the rights to Moran's idea and continued to open Save-a-Lot stores. In 1983, Wetterau, Inc., a local food wholesaler and retailer, bought General Grocer. In 1992, SUPERVALU, Inc., acquired Wetterau.

Today, with more than 1,150 stores across the country, Save-a-Lot is the nation's fifth largest retail grocery chain operating under a single banner and serves more than four million shoppers each week. Twenty-three of the stores are in the metropolitan area, and Save-a-Lot's headquarters is still in St. Louis. As for Bill Moran—he retired as president and chief executive officer in 2006 but serves as a consultant.

Shop 'n Save stores first opened in St. Louis in 1979. In 1983, Wetterau, Inc., bought the stores, and when SUPERVALU acquired Wetterau in 1992, the deal included all of them. Today, there are thirty-eight Shop 'n Save stores in the metropolitan area and three in Springfield, Illinois.

A LOOK AT PRODUCE ROW

Today, most of the big groceries have their own distribution warehouses. The rest, along with numerous other customers, turn to the St. Louis Produce Market, Inc., better known as Produce Row. Situated north of downtown, the huge wholesale market is a city within a city that has a culture, language, and customs of its own.

Every day, food from Produce Row feeds 4.5 million people within a three hundred-mile radius of St. Louis. Customers include many independent grocery stores and also the food suppliers who service groceries, restaurants, schools, hospitals, and nursing homes. The Saint Louis Zoo also is a customer, so next time you see Raja nibbling daintily on apples or bananas, know that the fruit came from Produce Row.

Top: An artist's sketch of Produce Row, made in 1953. Courtesy of Clarence Hughes.

Above: The real deal, photographed in the mid-1980s. Courtesy of Clarence Hughes.

Here is a look at Produce Row by the numbers:

- Number of companies: 27

- Number of employees: 1,100 to 1,800 (depending on the season)

- Footprint: 40 acres

- Number of buildings: Two, each 1,235 feet long and 115 feet wide

- Number of units: 98, each measuring 2,000 square feet

Distributors in forty-nine states (Alaska is the exception) and seventy-nine countries provide

CHARLES P. GALLAGHER, SR.:
IN THE SERVICE BUSINESS

United Fruit & Produce, located on Produce Row, is the largest produce wholesaler in the area. The company sells to groceries and restaurants and to those businesses that sell to groceries and restaurants.

Charles P. Gallagher, Sr., chairman of United Fruit & Produce, started in the business in 1959. Over the years, he has seen the wholesale produce business wax and wane and then come back yet again to thrive another day.

"We've been a success story only because we've had the vision to perpetually reinvent ourselves," says Gallagher. "As time goes on, as the population keeps growing, there will be more people living on the same amount of land who will require more service. That's what we do here—service."

The first threat to the business came in the late 1950s, when some of the bigger chain stores in town decided to set up their own warehouses and buy direct. "For about ten years, business was dragging," says Gallagher. "Then the independent stores and some of the national chains started to come here. That was a turning point to go forward again."

Then along came bagged lettuce—a change from fresh produce to processed produce. "We had been selling seven or eight truckloads of lettuce to a customer, and now we were selling maybe three," recalls Gallagher, "Around the same time—this was in the 1980s—people started eating out more, buying fewer groceries. The wholesale produce business was a sunset industry once again."

Guess what turned things around?

"Diets," says Gallagher.

"The cabbage diet, the grapefruit diet—all the diet programs worked it hard about vegetables and fruit, and that had a good effect. Before that, we used to sell a customer one load of broccoli. Suddenly, we were selling eight loads. Even the government got behind the call to eat more produce."

Another beneficial change has been the increased interest in more varieties of fruit. At one time, you could find only four varieties of apples in St. Louis: Red Delicious, Golden Delicious, Jonathan, and Rome. Granny Smith apples made an appearance in local groceries around 1980, and today, it's not unusual to see a dozen different varieties in stores.

Another development has long-term implications for the health of Gallagher's business. As the 1980s evolved into the 1990s, new customers started showing up at United Fruit & Produce: Asian restaurateurs and Asian grocery owners.

"They wanted napa cabbage, bok choy, snow peas," says Gallagher. "Always, we buy what sells—so, in response, we extended our inventory. At one time, we had maybe forty Asian vegetables. Now we have over five hundred."

Gallagher predicts that the children of those restaurateurs and grocery owners will build on their parents' success and continue to serve the community by opening a second or even a third grocery or restaurant. "And we will continue to offer them a place to buy food," says Gallagher.

---

products to Produce Row. Most fruit and vegetables are delivered by tractor trailers, or flown in. About 1 percent arrives by rail.

The wholesale market opened at its current location in 1953. Prior to that, vendors ran independent businesses near Third and Franklin, but there was no unified system for sellers or buyers. One of the early vendors was Henry Hollmann, who bought a potato-selling operation here in 1875. Barges on the Mississippi River brought in produce then, and it was off-loaded where Laclede's Landing is today.

In later years, 98 percent of the produce traveled to St. Louis by rail. In 1946, some 43,771 carloads of perishable foods came in on trains from forty states and two foreign countries, and two-thirds of that food was consumed here. Produce Row (which sits in an old railroad yard) and other wholesale operations like it in other cities were known as "terminal markets" because they were located near railroad terminals, where fresh fruit and vegetables could be stored on the grounds in refrigerated rail cars after arrival.

This undated photo shows a view of the early incarnation of Produce Row, at Third and Franklin. Courtesy of Clarence Hughes.

In those days, local "hucksters"—fruit and vegetable peddlers with horse-drawn wagons or trucks—arrived at Produce Row every morning by 5 a.m. to get the pick of the crop, and then made their way through the streets of St. Louis. Joseph Michael Corrigan was a huckster. "I remember helping my father sell strawberries in the summer," recalls his daughter, Betty Corrigan Dameris. "I'd go door to door, up and down the streets in our neighborhood, and I got to keep the money for any I sold."

With her background, Dameris might have gone on to be included in the book *Grocery Clerks Who Have Become Successful*, compiled in 1925 by Bartlett Arkell, president of the Beech-Nut Packing Company. Arkell's stated intention was to "inspire the million men and women" then in the business.

The book salutes twenty-eight men, including Edward Haas of Neosho, Missouri. Abraham Lincoln is the only well-known person in the book. Arkell recalls that the first job Lincoln had after leaving his father's home in 1831 was as a grocery clerk at Denton Offuts' store in New Salem, Illinois.

The chapter on Lincoln notes that he once overcharged a customer by 6 cents, and after the store closed for the day, Lincoln walked three miles to return the money. Honest Abe also was said to have inadvertently weighed tea on an inaccurate scale, and he reimbursed the customer after discovering the error. (Clearly, Lincoln would have made a sterling member of the St. Louis Grocery Clerks, but by the time the union was organized on April 18, 1886, the sixteenth president of the United States had been dead for over two decades.)

GROCERS OF YESTERYEAR

In 1898, the Adam Roth Grocery Company issued *A Story of Fifty Years: 1848–1898*, a booklet bound with a golden cord in commemoration of fifty years of doing business in St. Louis. The small booklet provides much insight into that era.

Born in 1826 in Hosbach, Germany, Adam Roth opened his first store here in 1848 in a sixteen-by-thirty-foot room at Fifth and Spruce. Roth slept in the back of the store, sharing the only bed with the grocery clerks and any customers in town from the country who needed a place to stay for the night before heading back home.

Here, directly from the pages of the booklet, is a thumbnail sketch of the grocery business in St. Louis in 1848, when the city had a population of 62,000:

- Business hours were from 5 a.m. to 10 p.m.
- Grocers made their own paper bags
- Brooms were made by the farmers who grew the corn
- Creameries and creamery butter were unknown
- There were no cold storage warehouses
- Matches were sold in bundles
- Smoking tobacco was sold from barrels
- Refined sugar came in large loaves that hung from the ceiling, and the sugar was sold in lumps
- Sand or corn meal was used as blotting paper
- Grocers put up their own pickles
- Few manufactured articles were sold
- Trademarked articles were almost unknown

In 1853, Roth tore down the existing building and erected a brick structure for his store. Next, he opened a wholesale grocery at 111 North Main. The first railroad service here began in 1856. Before that, the booklet notes, food came in—and went

Produce baskets await customers at G. A. Marsh Company, a vendor in the early days of Produce Row. Courtesy of Clarence Hughes.

out—on steamboats or in wagons pulled by teams of oxen.

During the Civil War, Roth put in place a generous policy: If a family had a relative in the war, wives and dependents did not have to pay until the war was over. After the war, Roth moved the wholesale business to Cupples Street, where he leased 40,000 square feet. Around this time, Roth also opened the Early Breakfast Coffee Company.

By 1898, Roth's retail grocery business filled an eight-story building. Also, he had developed the Squirrel Brand of canned goods, and he owned six delivery wagons. Roth operated in direct competition with Adolph E. Moll, the grocer who lured in customers with the 2,300-pound wheel of cheese from Sheboygan.

The Moll family also published a commemorative booklet celebrating fifty years in business. *The House of Moll: Fifty Successful Years (1858–1908)* begins with formal photos of the men of the Moll family. The last page of the booklet features a photo of a large orange cat identified as "Bill, who keeps the cellar free of rats and mice."

The pages in between tell the story of another grocer of yesteryear. In 1858, Adolph Moll, a twenty-five-year-old German immigrant, and Henry Heidsieck each invested $450 to open Heidsieck & Moll Groceries on Third Street between Market and Chestnut. Their venture was successful, and the store moved

GROCERY HISTORY AT A GLANCE

1930: Michael Cullen opens America's first supermarket in Queens, New York, and names it King Kullen. Also, the first line of retail frozen foods goes on display in Springfield, Massachusetts, with products manufactured under the Birds Eye brand.

1935: A $2,800 annual income puts a family of four in the middle class. Food claims one-fourth of the family budget at $700 a year.

1937: Sylvan Goldman of Oklahoma City invents the shopping cart. Also, Kraft Macaroni & Cheese is introduced, and nine million boxes are sold the first year at a cost of nineteen cents each. Today, more than one million boxes are sold every day.

1939: The first precooked, frozen meals are introduced by Birds Eye.

1946: The A&P grocery chain introduces the store-within-a-store concept by adding in-store bakery shops served from central bakeries.

1950: During the decade, the number of supermarkets more than doubles, from 14,000 in 1950 to 33,000 in 1960.

1953: Some 13 percent of fresh meat sales is now sold on self-service basis.

1954: C.A. Swanson & Sons introduces the frozen "TV" dinner in the first year that RCA markets the first color television sets.

1955: The home microwave is introduced.

1958: The Kroger Company introduces a service deli, bakery, and barbecue shop at a store in Detroit under the name "The Continental Counter." Also, the aluminum can makes its debut as a food container—for Parmesan cheese.

1962: Giant Food in Landover, Maryland, introduces the first in-store pharmacy.

1966: The Pillsbury Doughboy introduces prepared biscuit-dough products.

1969: Estimates are that 46 percent of the 55 billion pounds of fresh produce marketed annually are prepackaged prior to store delivery, up from 20 percent in 1955; 35 percent in 1958; and 40 percent in 1964.

1972: A tide of twenty-four-hour openings sweeps across the nation, raising a host of operating challenges at groceries.

1974: The first product is scanned on June 26—a pack of Wrigley's gum at Marsh Supermarkets in Troy, Ohio.

1976: Price Club, the first membership warehouse club, opens in San Diego, California.

1978: Generic private-label products begin appearing on supermarket shelves.

1981: Lean Cuisine is introduced.

1982: Diet Coke comes on the market.

1983: Safe-Strap Company introduces the first shopping cart seat belts.

1984: A prototype electronic shelf label system is introduced in a Dallas supermarket.

1988: The top five items that consumers use coupons for are cereal, dog food, cat food, coffee, and laundry detergent.

1991: Salsa sales in the United States surpass those of ketchup by $40 million.

1992: Whole Foods Market becomes the nation's first publicly traded natural foods supermarket company.

1994: Some 310 billion coupons are distributed, yet only 6.2 billion are redeemed.

1995: The Kroger Co. is the first supermarket to take grocery orders for home delivery via the Internet. The fee for the service is ten dollars on orders of less than one hundred dollars, and 10 percent of cost of orders exceeding one hundred dollars.

1997: From 1987 to 1997, the average number of different items sold in the supermarket produce department rises from 173 to 335.

2000: About 44 percent of weekday meals are prepared in thirty minutes or less. Ninety percent of supermarkets offer prepared foods—up from 84 percent in 1999.

2003: Consumers spend just 6.1 percent of their disposable income on food-at-home, compared to 1930, when consumers spent 21.2 percent of their disposable income on food-at-home.

2004: The low-carbohydrate diet craze peaks in February when 9.1 percent of Americans claim to be on the diet. By the end of the year, just 4.9 percent of adults are on the diet and sales of low-carb products fall off.

(Source: The Food Marketing Institute, the leading trade association representing food retailers and wholesalers around the country. For more fun food facts, see their website at www.fmi.org/facts_figs/?fuseaction=75_anniversary.)

In 1932, Moll's Grocery at Delmar and DeBaliviere boasted a tower clock designed in 1921 that now stands at North Second Street and Morgan on Laclede's Landing. Courtesy of Missouri History Museum, St. Louis.

to larger quarters at 620 Franklin in 1861, where it "took root and flourished like a green bay tree year after year."

In 1863, Heidsieck retired. Under Moll's supervision, the business grew, and Moll moved his store to increasingly larger properties. Like Roth, Moll also entered the wholesale grocery business and opened several warehouses. He also developed a house brand of canned goods called Delmar Club.

In its heyday, Moll's Grocery offered customers forty different teas, coffees, and cereals, and over one hundred relishes. The store specialized in "cakes, crackers, sugar-cured hams, smoked meats, and sausages." The booklet notes: "Eight phones bring in orders all day long. On an average day, 10,000 items are taken out to fill orders, and deliveries are made in horse-drawn carriages." The Moll stable housed sixty-seven horses and mules, thirty-five wagons, and six buggies.

Moll and his family claim to have revolutionized the checkout system. "Twenty five years ago the old-fashioned method of handling cash from customers was by cash buys, which was very slow and often unsatisfactory," states the booklet. "Today the cash is handled entirely on a system whereby the customer pays the cashier, rather than the salesmen in the departments." Imagine what the Molls would have thought of self-checkout lanes, which were installed in a handful of supermarkets in 1990!

Records show that in the late 1940s Moll's was still in business, with a store on Delmar at De-Baliviere. The store is long gone, but the tall tower clock designed in 1921 that once stood in front of Moll's now tells time at North Second Street and Morgan on Laclede's Landing.

From all accounts, Adolph Moll made it big in the grocery business. Historical records claim the grocer was "the forerunner of the present-day supermarket." The store's slogan says it all: "Moll's is one of the old familiar landmarks, well and favorably known to every man, woman and child in St. Louis."

That slogan applies to many a grocery here today.

THE HISTORY OF FOOD REGULATION AT A GLANCE

1941: South Carolina is the first state to mandate enrichment of white bread with vitamins and minerals.

1963: Senator Philip A. Hart (D-Michigan), sponsor of the "truth in packaging" bill, is indignant when an eight-inch pie contains only forty cherries. He requests that the Food and Drug Administration set standards on how many cherries a pie should contain.

1966: The "truth-in-packaging" law passes.

1970: Robert Choate, nutrition expert, tells a Senate subcommittee that breakfast cereals are not good sources of nutrition. The publicity prompts producers to fortify their products with vitamins and other nutrients.

1973: Nutrition labeling is standardized by the FDA in response to pressure from consumer groups.

1980: The Dietary Guidelines for Americans is released, providing the basis for the federal nutrition policy that affects nutrition assistance programs, including school lunch program and federal nutrition education messages.

1982: Manufacturers begin formulating their products to have less salt, in response to the nation's sodium problem.

1986: The Office of Management and Budget approves an FDA proposal allowing the use of irradiation on fruits and vegetables to control bacteria, insects, and other food contamination, and to extend product shelf life.

1990: The United States Department of Agriculture introduces the Food Guide Pyramid. Also, the Organic Foods Production Act gives the USDA power to create national organic certification standards, certify organic products, and set stiff fines and jail sentences for false labeling.

1992: Food irradiation begins in Florida with eleven hundred pints of strawberries.

1993: The Nutrition Labeling and Education Act takes effect in May. The law expands and clarifies nutrition information on thousands of products.

1996: The FDA approves Olestra, the first fat substitute, for use in snack foods such as chips and crackers.

1998: Irradiation of meat is approved by the FDA.

2002: On October 21, the national organic standards are fully implemented and products labeled "USDA certified organic" appear on shelves for the first time.

(Source: The Food Marketing Institute.)

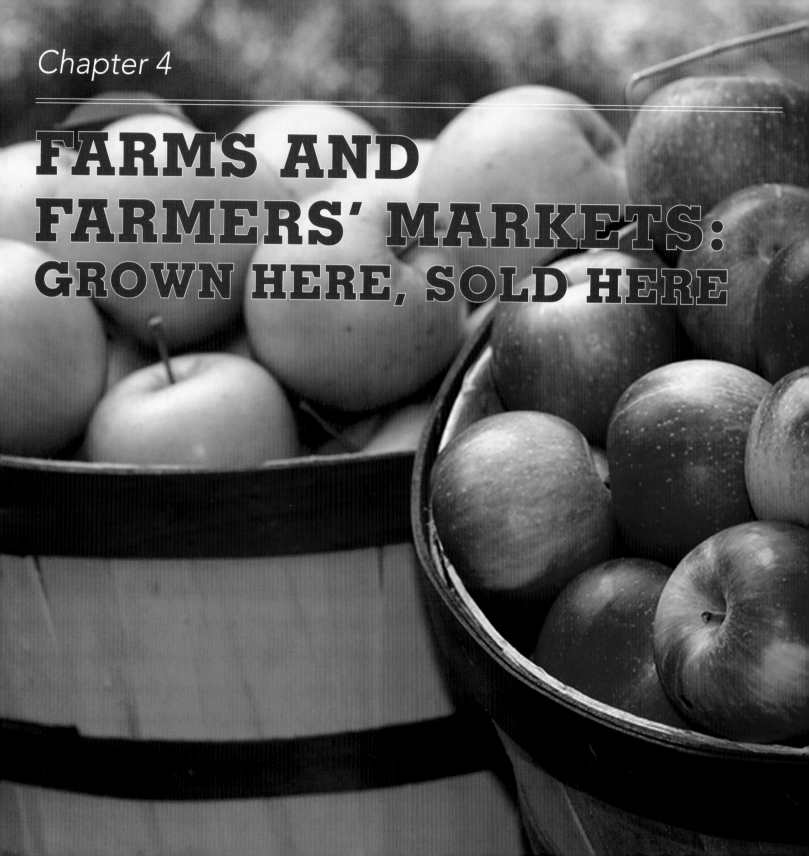

Chapter 4

FARMS AND FARMERS' MARKETS: GROWN HERE, SOLD HERE

What's this year's cash crop? Farmers' markets. The U.S. Department of Agriculture lists more than four thousand farmers' markets currently operating in the United States, up 18 percent from 2004. The markets provide revenue for farmers—more than nineteen thousand farmers told the USDA they sell their produce only at farmers' markets—and consumers have access to locally grown, farm-fresh produce and a chance to meet the farmers.

Tower Grove Farmers' Market. Courtesy of Sara Anne Finke.

"Every day, I get e-mails about new markets going in," reports Deb Connors, president of the Missouri Farmers' Market Association. "Every neighborhood now wants its own. Even shopping centers are putting in farmers' markets. Crown Center in Kansas City now has one."

Ten years ago, the Missouri Department of Agriculture listed sixty-three farmers' markets in their directory. Today, that list includes 135 scattered across the state. About a dozen are in the St. Louis metropolitan area.

What's up? "People want to know where their food comes from, and they want to know who is growing it," says Connors, who also serves as market master at the City Market in Kansas City. "That's not true just for organic produce but for all locally grown food. Right now, many people are more interested in buying food from small farmers in their area than from big growers somewhere across the country."

Patrick Horine, who with his wife, Jenny Ryan, founded the Tower Grove Farmers' Market in 2006, has a theory about the renewed interest in locally grown foods. "This moment is kind of a perfect storm," says Horine. "We've had bad food from China and salmonella from California. Gas prices are getting higher, and that means that soon local food will be cheaper. At the same time, lots of

Courtesy of Sara Anne Finke

books and articles have come out in support of locally grown and produced food."

Here's the deal: Food produced in the United States travels an average of 1,500 miles from "field to fork" and 400 gallons of oil are required to "make pesticides, fertilizer and animal feed, and to transport cattle and the like, to feed one person for one year," Roger Doiron said in the *New York Times* in April. Doiron is the founder of Kitchen Gardeners International, a nonprofit organization that counts more than five thousand individuals from ninety-six countries as virtual members.

Here is the same song, different verse: An apple picked and shipped more than six thousand miles from New Zealand has twice the negative impact on the environment as an apple grown in the Midwest. Tomatoes bred with thick skins can be picked by machines and travel long distances without bruising, but those tomatoes also can be deficient in vitamins, minerals, and antioxidants. Grapes grown in South America may be sprayed with pesticides that kill North American songbirds spending the winter in warmer climes. The bobolink population has declined by 50 percent over the last four decades.

Change likely will not come from any shame we may feel about making thoughtless decisions regarding food purchases, asserts Michael Pollan, author of *In Defense of Food: An Eater's Manifesto*. What will bring change? Higher food prices, says Pollan. In the *New York Times* this spring, Kim Severson reported that the Consumer Price Index puts food costs at about 4.5 percent more this year than last year. She explains why this delights "locavores, small growers, activist chefs," and Pollan, among others.

"Higher food costs, they say, could push pasture-raised milk and meat past its boutique status, make organic food more accessible and spark a national conversation about why inexpensive food is not really such a bargain after all," writes Severson. In the article, Pollan makes the point that higher food prices at supermarkets "level the playing field for sustainable food that doesn't rely on fossil fuels."

As Connors noted, the burgeoning growth of farmers' markets is a direct response to consumer demand. Horine says that in 2006, his market in Tower Grove drew about twelve hundred people a week. The following year, eighteen hundred showed up each Saturday the market was open, and he hoped for over two thousand people a week in 2008.

What do customers find at the Tower Grove Farmers' Market? "Our mission is all about local foods, about helping farmers, about what's good for the environment," says Horine. "Our long-term goal is to help improve the health of city residents, and already our surveys show that two-thirds of our customers are from the neighborhood. About half walk or bike to the market."

FARMERS GO TO MARKET

Vendors at the market all farm or operate ranches within 150 miles of here, and Horine and Ryan do not allow reselling. ("Resellers" buy produce from Produce Row or directly from big growers and sell the food at low prices at some farmers' markets.) Among the vendors at Tower Grove Farmers' Market through the season are:

- Biver Farms
- Centennial Farms
- City Seeds Farm
- Hinkebein Hills
- Kimker Hill Farm
- Live Springs Farm
- New Roots Urban Farm
- Norris Farms
- Our Garden
- Prairie Grass Farms
- ShowMe Fresh Produce
- Sunflower Savannah
- Three Rivers Community Farm

Other local vendors bring bread, baked goods, coffee, prepared vegetable salads, soup and dip mixes, fresh pasta, and crepes. "The most popular items are whatever is in season at the moment—strawberries, tomatoes, peaches. And our meat vendors do well, too, a nice steady business," says Horine.

Biver Farms displays fresh produce at the Tower Grove Farmers' Market. Courtesy of Biver Farms.

Courtesy of Biver Farms

Courtesy of Biver Farms

The Tower Grove Farmers' Market depends on donations to cover about half their costs, as it is the only market in the area that is not backed by a city government or large corporation. The Clayton Farmer's Market is sponsored by Straub's Markets, *Sauce Magazine*, and the city of Clayton. Founded in 1976 as a bicentennial project by the city of Kirkwood, the Kirkwood Farmers' Market now is owned by the city and run by a city-appointed committee and the Downtown Kirkwood Special Business District.

The Ferguson Farmers' Market, which operates on Saturdays at 20 South Florissant Road, also is a civic enterprise. "Teresa Carper started the market as a way to promote Ferguson and also to provide fresh vegetables and fruit for everyone," recalls Gunnar Brown, market master. Now in its sixth year, the market started small, with eight or nine farmers, but over the years, nearly thirty have been involved.

"Our market has a lot of camaraderie—and, of course, fresh vegetables and fruit, homegrown beef and pork, eggs, goat milk, some live chickens, and fresh butter and cheese," says Brown. "I always get greedy when the snow peas and sugar snaps come in. I buy too much, and then freeze some of them."

Among the vendors are Cascade Farms, Crooked Lane Farm, Garden Glen, Gibbs Greenhouse, Hahn Farm, Kamp's Orchard, Native Missouri Flowers, Our Garden, Pappardelles Pasta, Prouhet Vegetable Farm, "R" Pizza Farm, Seibert Farms, and Voss Pecans. Twice, the Department of Agriculture named the market "Missouri Farmers' Market of the Year," and it was named Best Farmers' Market 2007 by the *Riverfront Times*.

For Beth Thompson, participating in the Ferguson Farmers'

Market jumpstarted her new business, a bakery called *Cose Dolci*, at 100 South Florissant Road. "I started baking for the market that first year, using a certified kitchen to make cookies, scones, pound cake, and muffins," recalls Thompson. "I got a good following early on, and I opened my shop in December 2006. This was no midlife crisis. I'd always wanted to do this," she says. "And now I am."

The St. Louis Brewery sponsors the Maplewood Farmers' Market, held Wednesday evenings and some Saturdays at the Schlafly Bottleworks, 7260 Southwest Avenue. In its fifth year, the market draws more than a dozen farmers, in addition to other vendors.

Hally Bini, market coordinator, says she appreciates every farmer who participates. "Many people tend to romanticize farming, but it's a hard life," says Bini. "Before taking part in a market, farmers have to consider whether they will have enough business to make it worth the time to spend the evening in Maplewood. And right now, though the demand for local products is increasing, it's harder than ever for farmers to make ends meet."

Lane McConnell, a marketing specialist with the Missouri Department of Agriculture, addressed that issue earlier this year in a posting on her blog at http://mofarmersmarket.blogspot.com:

"Poultry, milk, meat and other agricultural products are increasing in cost, up about 5 percent in Missouri during the last few months. Farmers, however, are not the ones receiving a majority of the extra money consumers are spending. According to the USDA, farmers receive 22 cents of every dollar consumers spend on food (which is down from 47 cents in 1950 and 31 cents in 1980). The other 78 cents goes primarily for processing, packaging, transporting and retailing the food."

Lane notes that the 22 cents farmers receive is not clear profit. "Farmers use the proceeds from their sales to pay for fertilizer, fuel, farm machinery, and other expenses, some of which have increased 300 percent this decade alone. Only after these expenses are paid can farmers determine their profit. According again to USDA, 3.5 percent represents the average farmer's profit on all his gross receipts."

A PENNY FOR YOUR THOUGHTS

McConnell does the math and determines that less than a penny represents the farmer's profit. "This one cent is the farmer's 'take home pay' used to support a family, provide housing, pay for college, put food on the table, and pay for other living expenses."

Joanna Duley and Sam Hilmer operate Claverach Farm in Eureka, where they make organic wine and grow organic produce. "This is a really interesting time to be doing what we're doing," says Duley. "For the small farmers who have been in the business for the last ten or twelve years, the whole scene is still embryonic in terms of the community coming together around the markets. Also, in order to have a thriving market scene, you have to have more small farms—and this is an incredibly tenuous profession."

Duley lists the ongoing challenges: The weather, the expense, the time involved. "And it can be exhausting," she says. Duley earned an art degree at Washington University and promptly took a job as a professional baker and cook. As her interest in food developed, she started a garden and went to work for Paul Krautmann at Bellews Creek Farm. She started working with Hilmer seven years ago.

In the late 1800s, Sam Hilmer's great-grandfather bought property in what is now Clayton. He called his farm Claverach, which means "clover fields" in Welsh. Sam's grandfather also was a farmer. When Sam got out of college with a degree in anthropology, he started growing vegetables, says Duley. Now he works as vineyard manager and makes Claverach wines. Duley grows fresh produce as well as micro greens (three-to-four-inch-high leaves and stems from vegetables, flowers, or greens), including a wide variety of lettuces, spinach, chard, cress, and herbs.

"All of a sudden, the kind of thing we do is very much in the public eye," says Duley. "The paradox is that big agriculture is getting into organic, too, and now everybody wants a farmers' market in their neighborhood."

The Ferguson Farmers' Market offers everything from fresh produce to fresh-made salsas and relishes. Courtesy of Keith and Shannon Howard.

Courtesy of Keith and Shannon Howard

Courtesy of Joann Giuliani

That's not likely to happen, she says, for three reasons:

- Much of the farmland all over the country is being developed into suburbs
- Unless you are wealthy or already own farmland, it's very expensive to start a farm, even a small one
- To make any kind of profit, farmers need to sell out every week at farmers' markets

"People need to know that if they truly like the idea of buying from local farmers, they need to make a commitment to go to the market every week," she says. Claverach Farm takes part in the Maplewood Farmers' Market and the Clayton Farmer's Market.

Keith Biver and Brett Palmier from Biver Farms reserve spots at five farmers' markets: Edwardsville, Tower Grove, Clayton, Maplewood, and Kirkwood. If visions of warm, sunny mornings and swarms of eager shoppers clad in shorts and tee-shirts come to mind, consider this picture: Palmier at the Kirkwood Farmers' Market with a wool hat pulled over his baseball cap, shivering in a flannel shirt, gloved hands cradling a cup of hot coffee on a 45-degree morning in April, a brisk wind rising and frigid raindrops falling. That's part of the job, too.

Biver Farms is in Edwardsville, on forty acres that Biver's parents have owned since 1978. In both the Biver and Palmier households, the day starts about 7:30 a.m. "We both have kids to get off to day care, and then we work until about 5 or 6 p.m., both in the fields and on the bookkeeping," says Biver. "Our early days are Saturdays, when we have to get up about 4:30 a.m. and get the trucks loaded up for the markets."

Early in the season, as on that cold, gray day in Kirkwood, they sell potted herbs and vegetables. At the height of the season, Biver and Palmier sell organic produce. Last year, the cherry tomatoes and raspberries were the biggest sellers. "We started in 1996," says Biver, "and we've definitely seen more people at the markets each year since then."

A one-room log cabin, built in 1851, is on Biver's property. These historic homesteads are staples on many of the area's farms. Darrell Thies, who with his brother Dave owns Thies Farm, works land on North Hanley Road where his great-grandfather's home, built in 1888, once stood. "In the early days, every farmstead was self-contained," says Thies. "Everybody had cows, chickens, and turkeys, and there were horses and mules to work the fields. Times have changed."

Thies grows vegetables and fruit now but the biggest draw is his pumpkins. "Every year in October, we take up entertainment farming," says Thies. "We set up a one-acre playground called Pumpkinland, where everything is made of straw. We've got swings, slides, tunnels, a pirate ship, and a cornfield maze. We've also got farm animals, music, hayrides, and food."

DARRELL THIES: A FARMER'S LIFE

Darrell Thies, with his brother Dave, owns Thies Farm, one of the largest farms in the St. Louis area, with about 120 acres in Maryland Heights and another ten on North Hanley Road. Putting in sixty to seventy hours a week, Thies grows thirty food items using sustainable agriculture practices, mixing organic and non-organic methods and following guidelines from the extension services at the University of Missouri and the University of Illinois.

Young Darrell Thies. Courtesy of Thies Farm.

Along with flowers and plants, the food items are sold at farm stands on the premises, at 4215 North Hanley Road in St. Louis and at 3120 Creve Coeur Mill Road in Maryland Heights. Thies also sells to groceries and to some brokers, and he has taken part in the Ferguson Farmers' Market.

"Corn and tomatoes are our biggest retail items. Corn grows like crazy for us," says Thies. "We grow five acres of strawberries, and we have peaches and blackberries. We also have potatoes—yellow, white, blue, and red." Thies speaks eloquently about the flavor of a potato fresh from the ground, and then switches to a less tasty topic—the challenges every farmer faces.

Courtesy of Thies Farm

Among those challenges are the weather, government bureaucracy, the weather, competition that leads to oversupply, the weather, the immigration issue, and the weather. "Farmers always worry about the weather," says Thies on a rainy day. "We're never happy. Sometimes, we wish for rain, but today we'd like for it to quit."

Labor issues are a big problem this year, too. "I don't understand these opponents of amnesty. We've had immigrant families working for us for years, even through the second generation, and we've been forced to let go of those who are not documented," says Thies. "Now we can't find the workers we need. Not everybody wants to do what we do—we work in the cold and the mud and the rain."

In addition, new labeling laws now require Thies to put a sticker denoting origin on every tomato he sells to supermarkets. By spring 2008, Thies' labor costs were up 25 percent over last year. Fuel costs 40 percent more than last year, and fertilizer costs also were up 40 percent. On top of everything else, in a year Thies will move the farm in Maryland Heights. "We rented this land, and now it's under development," he says. "We're buying up land nearby, and we will build a new market stand."

A fifth-generation farmer, Thies pauses a moment to consider his situation. "Farming is hard work, and at times, it's hard to describe what it takes. But we love what we do."

At Eckert's Farms, entertainment farming is called "agri-tainment." Jill Eckert-Tantillo, vice president of Marketing and Food Services, says, "We draw our biggest crowds in late September and early October when the weather is perfect and people come to pick apples and pumpkins."

Seven generations of Eckerts have built their family business into the largest pick-your-own orchard operation in the United States. Eckert's owns farms in Belleville, Grafton, and Millstadt, and all three offer children's activities, annual events, and festivals. The Eckert's Country Store and Restaurant in Belleville is open daily and features locally grown food.

In 1837, Johann Peter Eckert came to Pittsburgh, Pennsylvania, from Germany with his wife and four sons. One of those sons, Michael, took up farming near Fayetteville, Illinois. His son, Henry, planted fruit trees in 1890 at Turkey Hill Farm, near Belleville. In 1910, Henry's son Alvin opened a roadside farm stand at Turkey Hill.

Today, Alvin's grandson Jim Eckert is president of Eckert Orchards and serves as chief horticulturist. Lary Eckert recently stepped down as president of Eckert's, Inc. Succeeding him is his son, Chris Eckert. Angie Eckert, Chris's wife, is vice president of retail operations for both the Country Store and the Garden Center.

Eckert's grows strawberries, blackberries, peaches, apples, and pumpkins. "We started our first pick-your-own program in 1964, in Grafton. At that time, pick-your-own was about getting the fruit cheaper than in the stores," says Eckert-Tantillo. "Now it's not so much about selling apples as is it is about selling the experience of coming to the farm, riding a tractor, listening to music, petting the animals, and spending a day in the country with your family. Today, it's about entertainment."

BEFORE GROCERY STORES

Entertainment farming likely would not have occurred to early St. Louisans. Throughout history, food has come from farms, and the people who worked those farms traded food for goods and arranged for needed services at the local market. In his plan devised in 1764 for the village of St. Louis, Pierre LaClede set aside a block of open field for a market. In his *Brief History of Public and Private Markets in the City of St. Louis*, Philip Taylor wrote that the first public market opened here in 1812. A map of the city prepared by Auguste Chouteau in 1825 shows the site, marked "La Place," bounded by Rue de la Tour (now Walnut), Rue de la Place (now Market), Grand Rue (now First Street), and the wharf.

Top: Visitors enjoy Pumpkinland at Thies Farm every October. Courtesy of Thies Farm.

Above: A petting zoo is part of the agri-tainment at Eckert's Farms. Courtesy of Eckert's Farms.

The first Public Market House was built on that site, and a picture of the building appeared on a ten-dollar bank note issued in 1817. Market days were Wednesdays and Saturdays, with buyers and sellers on the premises from daybreak to 10 p.m. Taylor notes that vendors caught selling goods outside the market were fined.

Responding to a growing population, the city later built North Market and South Market. The North Market, on the east side of Broadway between Lucas and Delmar, opened in 1832 and was one of the leading markets in the city. When it closed in 1868—a victim of westward expansion—the market's butchers flew the American flag at half-mast and draped the staff in mourning cloth before moving to Union Market, which the *St. Louis Home Journal* described at the time as "the splendid edifice just completed on Sixth Street."

William Carr Lane, the first mayor of St. Louis, authorized construction of a market on the riverfront, about where the Arch stands today. Inside that market was a two-story city hall. Lane served as mayor from 1823 to 1829, when about four thousand people lived here. He oversaw the first public health system in the city, opened free public schools, and was responsible for street improvements and for building fountains and planting greenery. Lane later served another term as mayor, from 1837 to 1840. By 1851, steamboats were bringing sugar, molasses, cotton, and tobacco to St. Louis. Cargo was unloaded on the levee, and goods were sold at local markets.

Other early markets in St. Louis were Lucas Market, Sturgeon Market, Mound Market, City Market, Central Market, South St. Louis Market, and Washington Market. The Biddle Market opened in 1856 on Fourteenth Street between Carr and Biddle, and vendors paid $3.75 a month to lease a stall. The market closed in 1957, and thirty years later, the City Health Department opened its Vector Control operation in the building.

Taylor notes that most markets were privately owned, and like today's farmers' markets, they also served as social centers. Most of them lasted a few years and then closed—with one notable exception.

FIRST MARKET HOUSE, 1812. (STONE.)
[*Drawn under direction of Fred. L. Billon.*]

Top: The first public market in St. Louis was a simple structure. Courtesy of the Library of Congress.

Right: The St. Louis riverfront was a busy place in the 1860s. Courtesy of the Library of Congress.

Facing: From all appearances, Sunday-best clothing was the norm while selling produce at local public markets. Courtesy of the Library of Congress.

SOULARD MARKET

Soulard Market, the third public market established in St. Louis, is the longest continuously operating market in the state and one of the oldest in the country. Philip Taylor, longtime market master, pays homage in *A Brief Description of Soulard Market, Past and Present*, written in 1975: "The market continues to operate, having survived through the Civil War, through a tornado which wrecked part of the building, through a depression, through neighborhood rehabilitation programs and through the construction of a new highway and a street widening which has left the market practically isolated, being surrounded on three sides by dead end streets."

At 730 Carroll Street, Soulard Market thrives even today.

On June 21, 1838, Julia Cerre Soulard, widow of St. Louis's surveyor general under the Spanish regime, set aside a meadow the size of two city blocks to be used as a public market. The market typically drew three to four hundred

farmers in wagons and with pushcarts, all aligned in two concentric circles with room for shoppers in between. In 1841, Soulard sold the meadow to the city with the stipulation that it remain a public market.

Two years later, farmers and vendors raised enough money to erect a one-story brick building to house perishable goods. Produce continued to be sold outside. Among the farmers at the market was Ulysses S. Grant, who sold cordwood cut from his land. Over the years, the building was expanded. On May 27, 1896, a tornado roared through town, killing forty, injuring nearly one hundred, and leveling buildings in an area two miles wide and three miles long. The Soulard Market building lost its second story in the storm.

In 1923, St. Louisans approved a bond issue for $87.4 million of city improvements, the largest of its kind in an American city. Soulard Market got an all-new building, a two-story brick structure designed by city architect Albert Osbury to resemble a foundling hospital in Florence, Italy, built in 1419 by the Renaissance sculptor and architect Filippo Brunelleschi. The building was dedicated on May 8, 1929, and the new, improved Soulard Market opened the next day.

Today, Soulard is open year-round, with some ninety vendors selling such items as barbecue sauce, beverages, bread, baked goods, candles, cosmetics, dairy products, ethnic foods, flavorings and seasonings, flour, fish, fresh vegetables and fruit, plants, honey, jellies and jams, meats, mushrooms, nuts, pasta, rice, poultry, and eggs. Vendors also offer decorative items, imported goods, unusual clothing,

Julia Cerre Soulard (inset) donated land for Soulard Market, shown here in this undated photograph. Courtesy of Missouri History Museum, St. Louis.

Facing top: In its hey day, Union Market was considered a "splendid edifice." This photograph shows stall 130—Caito and A. Busalaki. Courtesy of Missouri History Museum, St. Louis.

Facing bottom: Soulard Market exudes architectural dignity. Courtesy of Deborah Franke.

THE MANTIAS: SERVING PRODUCE VENDORS

For more than a half-century, the William Mantia Fruit Company was bananas. Literally. Sicilian immigrant Michael Mantia established the family trade in the early twentieth century. Wheeling a cart to the riverfront, Michael anticipated barges that carried and off-loaded produce. He would park his cart and await the delivery of bananas, just bananas.

The real scramble happened after pick-up; Michael and other wholesalers peddled their wares at the terminal markets at Third and Franklin Streets. A chaotic environment and disorganization prevailed there, but the surviving wholesalers reaped reward in the 1950s, when the government claimed the land for the construction of the Martin Luther King Bridge.

Displacement proved a blessing. A new entity formed: St. Louis Produce Market, Inc. It collected wholesalers who sought a more effective market operation. With the support of financing from railroad companies, the group built Produce Row in north St. Louis off Broadway—a 196,000-square-foot, two-building facility designed for efficiency and functionality.

From its opening in February 1953, Produce Row dramatically improved viability for its wholesalers. In Mantia's case, ease of distribution helped the company field banana deliveries from Guatemala, Honduras, and Colombia, all with minimal spoilage. Being part of Produce Row also enabled, and still enables, the William Mantia Fruit Company to serve a broad base of predominantly independent clients—from Soulard Market vendors to grocers without the means enjoyed by major chains.

That's not to say companies like Mantia could survive alone on the advantages afforded by the market and its system. The lifeblood that coursed through generations of Mantias waned in the 1990s. A steady decline in sales of the company's main product forced adaptation. The answer: Diversification. "Cousin Lou [Mantia] started by adding potatoes and onions," explained John Mantia, one of the current principals. "We gained expertise about different produce and recognized that clients like to get as much as they can in as few stops as possible."

Mantia Fruit Company still is bananas—but not just bananas. Greens, citrus, and other varieties of produce now are stocked alongside the bananas in refrigerated units at

John and Vince Mantia. Courtesy of Josh Stevens.

Courtesy of Josh Stevens

Mantia Fruit Company. None of it stays in place for long. Product is in constant flow, especially from April to August when the company operates around the clock.

With produce coming in or going out, the bill of lading still bears the name Mantia. Brothers John and Vince—alongside cousin Tony and faithful employees Mark Aguado and Mike Bergee—ply a trade learned from their father Gus, grandpa Michael, great uncle William, uncle Tony, and cousins Martin and Lou. The company endures, just as Produce Row endures. Perpetuating the role of independents in the industry. Replenishing markets with succulent produce. Flourishing.

and jewelry. Many of the vendors have been selling at the market for several generations.

"Soulard Market does not claim to be a true farmers' market. We are a public market," says Sandra Zak, market master. "Some people come because it's a tradition in their family, some come for the entertainment, and many people tell us they come here for the prices." Zak added that the market is fortunate to have great bakeries, meat producers and meat resellers, and fish. "It's easy to come to Soulard and pick up a lot of stuff so you don't have to make a trip to the supermarket."

Resellers make fruit and vegetables available all year 'round at Soulard, and some local farmers sell fresh produce in season. "A lot of farmers' markets have sprung up lately, and that's good," says Zak. "Everybody needs to support local farmers."

HELPING FARMERS HELP US

In the 1860s, 80 percent of Americans lived on farms. In Missouri, farmers produced corn, hay, barley, wheat, oats, grapes, and apples, and they raised hogs, cattle, horses, and mules. The Missouri State Board of Agriculture was founded in 1865, and five years later, the School of Agriculture at the University of Missouri–Columbia accepted its first students. Today, corn and soybeans are the big crops in Missouri.

According to the Agricultural Census of 2002, there were 106,797 farms in Missouri spread over 29,946,035 acres, down from 110,986 farms in 1997 on 30,202,772 acres. In 2002, St. Louis County had 328 working farms encompassing 39,395 acres with a market value of $166,115,000 producing crops and products with a market value of $21,266,000. That same year, 739 farms in St. Charles County produced products with a market value of $33,638,000.

Here's the story on vegetables: In 1950, 782 farms in St. Louis County grew vegetables on 6,091 acres. In 2002, vegetables were grown on just twenty-four farms and land set aside to cultivate farm-fresh produce was down to 307 acres. Orchards are disappearing, too. In 2002, twelve farms had a combined total of thirty-seven acres of orchards, compared to 1950, when orchards covered 2,215 acres on 1,094 farms.

"In the larger scheme of things, farms are producing more from every acre than ever before," says Gene Danekas, director of agricultural statistics for the USDA in Missouri. "From 1997 to 2002, we lost 4 percent of farms and 1 percent of acres, and yet last year this country produced 13.1 billion bushes of corn,

Top: Ulysses S. Grant built Hardscrabble, a four-room cabin, on his farm here in 1856. Courtesy of the Library of Congress.

Above: Some ninety vendors ply their wares at Soulard Market. Courtesy of Deborah Franke.

which is the most corn ever produced in the history of the United States." The 2007 production was 11 percent greater than the previous largest production, experienced in 2004, and nearly five times the amount produced in 1950.

Danekas zeroes in on corn production in Missouri: "In 1950, we produced 169 million bushels of corn on four million acres, with an average yield of forty-four bushels per acre. In 2007, we produced 462 million bushels of corn on 600,000 fewer acres, with a yield of 142 bushels per acre. Are there fewer farms? Yes, but we are producing more from the acres we have. Our producers are much more efficient than in the past, and we're raising more food than ever."

Bryan and Christina Truemper own Farrar Out Farm in Frohna, Missouri, about ninety miles south of St. Louis. They raise certified naturally grown produce, pasture-raised Berkshire pigs, sheep, rabbits, eggs, chickens, ducks, geese, and broadbreast and heritage-breed turkeys.

"I've learned you can make a living off a small diversified farm," says Bryan Truemper. "I've cooked full time at different restaurants in south St. Louis and Cape Girardeau, and I learned to like really good food. Then I moved to Maine, where I cooked at a lodge. My wife got a job at an organic farm, and I worked there part time. They sold what they grew at a farm stand there. This exposure to small-scale agriculture really opened my eyes."

In 2001, the Truempers moved to his grandparents' farm, where Bryan had spent many a summer while growing up. Their first year, they grew produce on one-third of an acre and raised two hundred chickens and twenty turkeys. Now, they grow produce on three to four acres, and they have about one thousand chickens as well as the other birds and animals. "My grandmother, Adelma Mueller, is from nearby Farrar—a speck of a town—and she helps us out. She picks green beans and washes eggs," he says.

The Truempers, who have two young children, sell their food at the Kirkwood Farmers' Market. "We've been at the market since 2004, and our business has doubled every year. With the economy as rocky as it is, buying locally will continue to build," says Truemper. Chicken, eggs, and pork are his big sellers, "our bread and butter," and he sells those year 'round. "We process the meat at our farm, and we bring it, all butchered and dressed, to St. Louis," says Truemper

Top: Pigs at Farrar Out Farm. Courtesy of Bryan and Christina Truemper.

Above: Small-scale agriculture appeals to Bryan and Christina Truemper, who own Farrar Out Farm. Courtesy of Bryan and Christina Truemper.

Farrar Out Farm also sells to area restaurants, including Five Bistro, at 4317 Manchester Avenue. "What is the point of buying a tomato in December," asks Anthony Devoti, chef and owner. "Why not use fresh products that are available to make a beautiful meal?"

Devoti, who grew up in Chesterfield, says he learned that from Judy Rodgers while working at Zuni, her restaurant in San Francisco. (Rodgers grew up in Kirkwood.) "I decided when I was fifteen or sixteen to be a cook," says Devoti. After high school, he spent some time backpacking in Europe. He traveled through Paris, Milan, and Antwerp, where he would go to farmers' markets every Wednesday and Saturday to buy food.

When he returned to St. Louis, Devoti enrolled in the culinary program at St. Louis Community College at Forest Park. He then attended the French Culinary Institute in New York, where once again Devoti spent time in public markets.

"When I came back to St. Louis, I was really interested in doing local food, and I talked that up everywhere I worked," says Devoti. "I got really frustrated. Only a handful of people were doing that here—Lou Rook, Eddie Neill, and Andy Ayers. I thought about going to New York or San Francisco or Portland, but I decided to stay here."

Devoti opened Five in June 2006. (He also owns the Newstead Tower Public House, at 4353 Manchester.) In mid-April this year, Devoti proudly declared that within the next three weeks 80 percent of his menu at Five—with the exception of some nuts and fish—would originate no farther than 130 miles from St. Louis.

"This year, we are going to begin a massive pickling project, putting up vegetables and making jams for winter with food from Farrar Out Farm, from Claverach Farm, and from others," he says. "This is the way people have eaten in Europe for hundreds of thousand of years."

Sticking to his principles on the matter of buying locally is a bit of a risk, but Devoti is adamant. "We live in the breadbasket of the United States. There is no reason why we shouldn't eat grains, breads, and meat in winter, and vegetables in spring and summer. Already, some people come here because of what we do and what we stand for. Others are still unsure, but eating locally is a huge thing for us as a city."

Top: Greenhouses and fields bring forth fresh food at Biver Farms in Edwardsville, where Keith Biver and Brett Palmier work forty acres that Biver's parents have owned since 1978. Courtesy of Biver Farms.

Above: Bryan Truemper, a former chef, is now at home on a tractor. Courtesy of Bryan and Christina Truemper.

THE SERMON ON FARMS AND FARMERS' MARKETS

Devoti is preaching to the choir when it comes to Andy Ayers, longtime owner of Riddle's Penultimate in the University City Loop. Ayers opened his first place with his wife, Paula, on Natural Bridge just east of Hanley Road in 1980. "I used to go up the street to the Thies Farm produce stand to buy homegrown tomatoes for myself and my family to eat while ordering in cases of 'Styrofoam' tomatoes to serve at the restaurant," recalls Ayers.

"That's the way I learned the restaurant biz: Late every evening check your stocks, call your guy on Produce Row, and next morning everything comes off the one truck. I remember well the day that Paula said, 'Don't you think our customers would like it if we served these good tomatoes?' Duh! I was like Saul, on the road to Damascus. An epiphany!"

Andy Ayers. Courtesy of Jonathan Pollack.

Right away, Ayers added a homegrown tomato salad to his menu. Later that first summer, he bought locally grown bi-color sweet corn and raspberries, and he made pies using real pumpkins. Today, Ayers had eighty farmers' names on file, and last year, he bought most of what he needed from twenty of them. ("Bought" is the operative word, because early in 2008, Ayers sold Riddles Penultimate to his daughter, Kate, but there is no reason to believe this particular policy will change.

"My ballpoint pens say 'Local food—good politics and good eatin' too!' If you want to use the best ingredients in your restaurant, they are in-season, locally grown ingredients," says Ayers. "The only way to get a real, tree-ripened peach is to buy from someone who is really dedicated to growing them, and does so very near your location."

So much for the good eatin'—now for the politics, a topic dear to Ayers' heart.

"It is terrifyingly bad public policy to concentrate the nation's food production in the hands of a few large corporations. The food quality is degraded and the environmental damage and petrochemical use is unsustainable," says Ayers. "I like farmers. I identify with their business model: Mom, Pop, the kids, and the hired hands is how I've always run my restaurant. They are entrepreneurs of the first order and invariably fascinating people."

Ayers pauses, and continues, "The rural countryside is endangered—the land and the people—along with the public health if we don't do something to buttress the small-scale rural economy. The solution is amazingly simple and close at hand: Buy their stuff. If we don't, they'll be gone."

Enough said—head for a farmers' market or farm stand today.

THE FARMERS' MARKET AS A DESTINATION

People go to farmers' markets to buy fresh produce, right? Sure—but that's not all.

"You should see the farmers' market in Raleigh-Durham—you could spend half a day there and not see everything," enthuses Kathy Noelker, the market director for the Ferguson Farmers' Market. After just one month on the job, Noelker already had her goal in mind. "I am promoting our market as a destination, and I am intent on getting families and children there every Saturday."

In April, Noelker was plotting out a calendar of special events, including live music, cooking demonstrations by local chefs, trail rides, a petting zoo, visits from a storyteller, and art activities. Picnic tables at the market provide a place for people to sit and linger.

In addition to farmers, the Ferguson Farmers' Market also invites local crafters and artisans to set up shop, selling handmade soap, purses, jewelry, botanical skincare products, pottery, Peruvian handicrafts, beads, and more, with new offerings each week. One new vendor is Hellenbush der Bauernhof from outside Hermann, which sells all-natural alpaca fiber and organic yarn.

The Land of Goshen Community Market in Edwardsville offers live entertainment and craft demonstrations every Saturday. Live music is part of the Maplewood Farmers' Market, where Brick City Gardens and Schlafly Bottleworks also offers "Good Gardening—Good Food," a series of organic gardening workshops, films, and lectures. (For more information, see www.schlafly.com/goodgardenseries.shtml.) On market nights, the menu at the Bottleworks often includes a dinner special that features farm-fresh produce.

The Maplewood Farmers' Market also teams up once a month for a special event with Slow Food St. Louis, the local branch of an international organization founded in 1989 whose aim is "to protect the pleasures of the table from the homogenization of modern fast food and life."

Special events at the Tower Grove Farmers' Market include music concerts, free yoga classes, a Green Living series for visitors to learn about sustainability, a 5K Walk/Run, talks on the politics of food, and cooking contests. In 2008,

Courtesy of Keith and Shannon Howard

the market also planned to introduce the Tower Grove Farmers' Market Kitchen Incubator, a commercial kitchen space where start-up food businesses can begin to develop their products and eventually sell those products at the market.

At Soulard Market, street musicians play on Saturdays, and snack bars in the market and restaurants in the neighborhood serve lunch. Food is a big draw at the St. Jacobs Farmers' Market near Waterloo. Vendors sell their wares both indoors and out, and hungry shoppers can taste both international favorites and local delicacies including sausage, apple fritters, and pure maple syrup sold by Mennonite farmers who travel to market by horse and buggy.

Chapter 5

RAISE A GLASS:
BREWERIES, WINERIES, AND WATERING HOLES

First in booze, first in shoes, last in the American League—so goes the old saying about St. Louis. More of a slam at the St. Louis Browns than a salute to two leading industries, the saying does serve as a reminder that any book about the culture of food in St. Louis also needs to offer up commentary on beverages. (The shoes we leave to another time, another tome...)

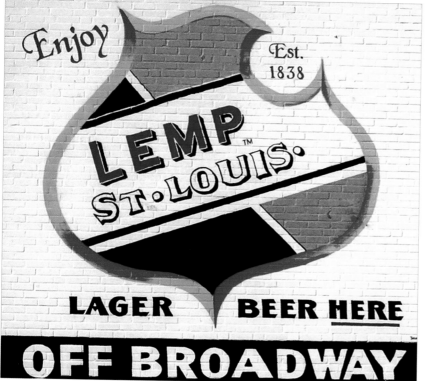

Courtesy of Matthew Heidenry

Previous Page: The St. Louis campus of the King of Beers. Courtesy of Anheuser-Busch Companies.

After all, the King of Beers keeps the primary castle here, on one hundred acres just south of downtown. In St. Louis alone, Anheuser-Busch had a brewing capacity of 15.8 million barrels in 2007. Add that to the output of the company's eleven additional breweries in the United States and several more overseas, and the company cooked up more than 128 million barrels in 2007, or enough to fill 50,000 Olympic-sized swimming pools.

Other royals, in the form of microbreweries, also are in residence. The Brewers Association, which promotes craft beers and brewers, reports that craft beer industry sales have grown 31.5 percent over the last few years. That may explain why brewpubs are popping up all over town.

If you prefer a bottle of wine to a bottle of beer, you will be pleased to learn that in 1980, the federal government saw fit to designate tiny Augusta, Missouri—under an hour's drive from St. Louis—as the first official wine district in America. Today, seventy-six wineries are sprinkled throughout the state, offering something for every taste.

Countless bars (far more than seventy-six!) serve as friendly "watering holes" in neighborhoods throughout the metropolitan area, but it turns out that we head for the corner tavern for other reasons, too. We meet friends there, we hang out, we watch sports—we even play sports at some bars, everything from darts to pinball to bocce. And some people get married in taverns, where it's just steps from the ceremony to the reception.

So sure, we like to eat—but we want something to wash the food down!

BREWERIES

Beer drinkers in St. Louis owe a hearty *danke schön* (that's "thanks") to the German immigrants who settled in our fair city. Yes, St. Louis was first settled by the French in 1764, who soon were joined by the Spanish, Indians, and blacks (both slaves and free men). By 1840, about 17,000 people lived here. Over the next two decades, the population swelled to 160,000, and German immigrants accounted for nearly one-third of the residents of St. Louis.

The Germans brought with them food, drink, and entertainment. Suddenly St. Louis "was inundated with breweries, beer houses, sausage shops, Apollo gardens, Sunday concerts, Swiss cheese, and Holland herrings," writes Maureen Ogle in her book *Ambitious Brew: The Story of American Beer.* "Nowhere, claimed one observer, had 'the German influence been more . . . beneficially felt, than in the introduction of beer.'"

The history of breweries in St. Louis is complex, with individuals opening up shop, entering into partnerships or working relationships with other brewers, then breaking off and starting new breweries. Untangling the history is as difficult as sorting out the connections among the Italian families in the restaurant business here—it's enough to drive you to drink.

Maybe that was the idea . . .

The Lemp Mansion

St. Louis, Missouri, Circa 1892

FIRST ONE OUT OF THE BREWHOUSE

In the early 1840s, Johann Adam Lemp, a native of Eschwege, Germany, left the grocery business and opened Lemp's Western Brewery, the first brewery in St. Louis, just about where the Gateway Arch now stands. Lemp and his son made just twelve barrels a year, and they made lager beer. Some historians say it was the first lager made in America; others give the credit to a fellow in Philadelphia. Either way, it was a bold new step—lager was unknown in this country—and it dramatically changed how beer was made in the United States.

The term "lager," we learned at www.schlafly.com, comes from the German verb *lagern*, which means "to stock" or "to store." In Germany, brewers aged their beer in caves, which are cool all year long. Lucky for the German immigrants eager to make beer here, the metropolitan area has many natural limestone caves.

Lemp later bought property that sat over the entrance to a cave near what is now the northwest corner of Cherokee and De Menil Place. He excavated the cave to a depth of over fifty feet,

PATTY POINTER: EERIE ECHOES FROM THE PAST

Back in the 1850s, the Lemp family was known nationwide for its beer, and their brewery was one of the largest in St. Louis. Today, the family's mansion gets all the attention—as one of the ten most haunted places in America.

Ghost hunters come from around the country hoping to hear or see something—anything—that would lend credence to the tales about deceased members of the Lemp family hanging out, as it were, in their old "haunt"—the thirty-three-room mansion at 3322 De Menil Place.

The Lemp Mansion has been featured on many national television shows and also in several books about haunted houses. What have people reported seeing and hearing in the house? Glasses flying off the bar, pianos playing in empty rooms, and a general sense of being watched.

"There are a lot of odd occurrences here," says Patty Pointer, whose family owns the mansion, which is now a bed and breakfast, a restaurant, a banquet center, and home to a mystery dinner theater.

"Doors open and close, faucets turn off and on, the phones go on hold all of a sudden," says Pointer. "A lot that happens could be explained away, but there definitely is something unexplainable within this house—and there has been a lot of tragedy here."

Here are some of the spirits said to be responsible for the unexplained disturbances:

- In 1901, Frederick Lemp died at age twenty-six of a heart attack

- Despondent over his son's death, William Lemp, Sr., shot himself in the head three years later

- In 1920, Elsa Lemp Wright, another of William's children, shot herself in the head

- William Lemp, Jr., shot himself in the heart two years after his sister's death

- In 1943, William Lemp, III, died of a heart attack at the age of forty-two

- A few years later, the illegitimate son of William Lemp, Jr., died in his thirties

- In 1949, Charles Lemp, a brother of Elsa and William, Jr., shot his Doberman Pinscher and then himself

"Sixty to 70 percent of the people who come here say they sense something," says Pointer. "Of course, we always tell guests that we can't guarantee anything. If we did, well—that would be like Disneyland."

Lemp Mansion. Courtesy of Matthew Heidenry.

twenty feet wide, and one hundred yards long, where he stored the beer made at his brewery. By the 1850s, Lemp was producing about five thousand barrels a year and operating a popular saloon that sold only his products.

In her book, Maureen Ogle notes that Julius Winkelmeyer's Union Brewery was much larger than Lemp's and one of the largest in the nation. Located on Market Street between Seventeenth and Eighteenth Streets, the Union Brewery produced about 15,000 barrels a year. Other breweries were in the neighborhood as well. "A mile or so south on Eighteenth stood the Phoenix Brewery, the city's second largest operation," writes Ogle. And nearby was Joseph Uhrig's Camp Spring Brewery, which boasted a popular beer hall and a ballroom.

The Bavarian Brewery, on the south side of the city, was owned by Eberhard Anheuser, an immigrant from Bad Kreuznach, Germany, who had made a fortune manufacturing soap. In 1860, he entered the brewing business by default, acquiring the brewery as payment for a debt. Enter Adolphus Busch—a native of Mainz, Germany, who married Anheuser's daughter, Lilly. Shortly thereafter, Busch joined his father-in-law in the beer-making business.

In 1862, Adam Lemp died and left the Western Brewery to his son William Jacob Lemp and his grandson Charles Brauneck. The partnership lasted two years. After serving in the Union Army, William Lemp built a new brewery near Thirteenth and Cherokee. In 1880, Anton Griesedieck, the son of a brewer in Stromberg, Germany, was ready to get in on the burgeoning business in St. Louis. (As noted at www.gb-beer.com, "a barrel of beer that cost a dollar to make could be sold for seven times that amount.") He bought the Phoenix Brewery.

By the early 1870s, some thirty breweries were operating in St. Louis, and Lemp's Western Brewery led them all in production. Within twenty years, the brewery was the first in the country to distribute its beer across the nation, and by the late 1890s, Lemp's beer enjoyed an international reputation. (At the time, Pabst beer, made in Milwaukee, ranked tops in sales in the United States.)

Around this same time, a group of English businessmen decided to create a "trust" (read "monopoly") and buy up all the breweries in St. Louis. They were able to make deals with just eighteen—including Hyde Park, Green Tree, and Wainwright—and they called their mega-company the St. Louis Brewing Association. The Griesedieck family sold their Phoenix Brewery to the trust for an inflated price and gleefully opened a new brewery, the National Brewing Company, at Eighteenth and Gratiot.

The combined efforts of Adolphus Busch (top left) and Eberhard Anheuser (top right) resulted in the world-renowned Anheuser-Busch Companies. Above is a view of the brew house from the early 1900s. Courtesy of Anheuser-Busch Companies.

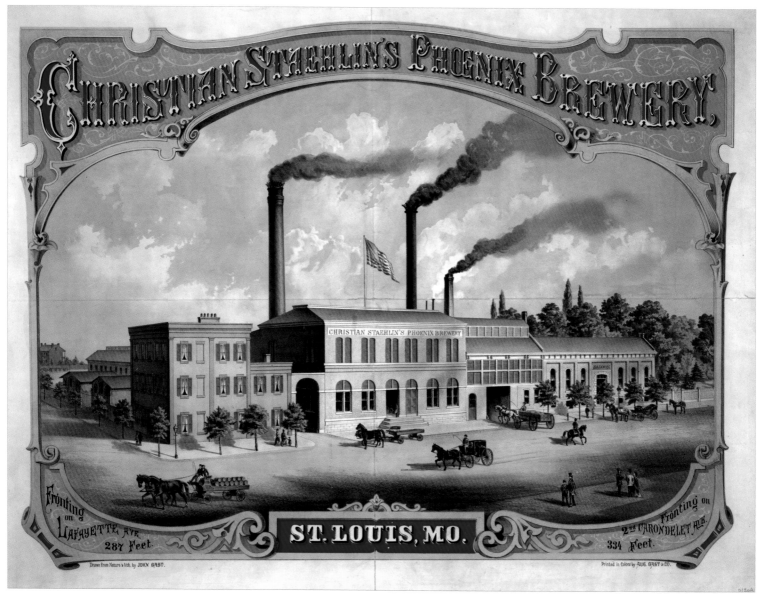

CHRISTIAN STAEHLIN'S PHOENIX BREWERY

CHRISTIAN STAEHLIN'S PHOENIX BREWERY

Fronting on LAFAYETTE AVE. 287 Feet.

ST. LOUIS, MO.

Fronting on 2ND CARONDELET AVE. 334 Feet.

Drawn from Nature & lith. by JOHN GAST.

Printed in Colors by AUG. GAST & CO.

RAY GRIESEDIECK: WHAT WAS OLD IS NEW AGAIN

If you don't try, you'll never know.

That's what Ray Griesedieck's mother, Libby Switzer Griesedieck, said when he asked her whether he should try to bring back Griesedieck Brothers beer, a beer that slaked America's thirst for almost a century.

And so Griesedieck tried, along with his cousins Alvin "Buddy" Griesedieck, III, and Stephen Butler. In 1992, Ray Griesedieck set up the corporation. By 2000, he and his cousins were officially the owners of Griesedieck Brothers Brewing Corporation. In 2002, they launched their first product, made at a microbrewery in St. Charles. Today, the beer is brewed by Sand Creek Brewing Company in Black River Falls, Wisconsin.

Griesedieck Brothers' packaged Golden Pilsner is now available in groceries and liquor stores, and on tap at a number of restaurants. "Our recipe is not the same American-style lager we had before," says Ray Griesedieck. "We're making a German pilsner, brewed under the German purity laws." The company also makes a Bavarian wheat beer, available only on tap.

Because Griesedieck is using the family name, he and his cousins hope to pique the curiosity of former customers. "We want to capture some of our old customers and also find new customers, and let them all experience what a German pilsner should taste like," he says. "Older customers tend to be loyal to one brand, but the new beer drinker moves around, tries a bunch of different products, just like wine drinkers."

Griesedieck's father was the last president of the original Griesedieck company, located at 1920 Shenandoah Avenue. "As a kid, I'd go to the brewery with my dad on Saturday mornings. In the office, I'd play with rubber stamps, and then I'd go for a ride on the forklift around the warehouse," he recalls. "I've always wanted to be in this business but never had the opportunity."

Now, with a push from his mother, he does—and what was old is new again.

BIG AND BIGGER

By the turn of the century, the Lemp family's Western Brewery was among the largest breweries in the country. Another brewery in St. Louis was even bigger. That brewery was Anheuser-Busch, where 3,500 employees brewed 6,000 barrels and shipped nearly 700,000 bottles of beer every day, all from an area that covered sixty city blocks.

Today, the world headquarters for Anheuser-Busch is still south of downtown St. Louis, on Pestalozzi Street, and the company is the leading brewer in the United States. How did that happen? What follows is a brief look back.

In 1864, Adolphus Busch went to work for his father-in-law, Eberhard Anheuser. That's true—but the company says there is no truth to the rumor that German monks shared their beer recipe and some brewer's yeast with Busch, who allegedly preserved the original strain of yeast in an ice cream freezer, using it for 140 years.

Anheuser and Busch increased their production and expanded sales beyond Missouri and into Texas and Louisiana, where "cowboys reportedly deserted their beloved red-eye whiskey for the light Bohemian-style beer" the brewers produced.

In the 1870s and 1880s, the company used innovations in the brewing industry—such as pasteurization, the invention of refrigerated railroad cars, and a coordinated system of rail-side icehouses—to increase distribution. As a full partner, Adolphus Busch took on greater responsibilities for the operation of the brewery. In 1876, the company debuted Budweiser, and twenty years later, Anheuser-Busch introduced Michelob. Ambitious national advertising campaigns resulted in Budweiser quickly becoming the most popular beer in the country.

In 1907, in response to increased competition from Anheuser-Busch and the St. Louis Brewing Association, nine local breweries—including Griesedieck, Columbia, Gast, and ABC Brewery—merged to become the Independent Breweries Company. (The merger was not successful, though one product remains on the market today: IBC Root Beer, originally developed during Prohibition.)

ANHEUSER-BUSCH CLYDESDALES: WHOA!

Legend has it that on April 7, 1933—the day beer became legal after Prohibition—August A. ("Gussie") Busch, Jr., encouraged his father, then the president of Anheuser-Busch, to have a look at the new vehicle he had bought. When the two stepped outside, there was a new Studebaker beer wagon and a six-horse hitch of magnificent Clydesdale horses.

That shiny new beer wagon was then loaded with the brewery's first cases of post-Prohibition beer, and the Clydesdales headed down Pestalozzi Street in celebration. The jubilant reaction from the public was such that the Busches sent the team and wagon by train to New York City, where the horses paraded down Thirty-fourth Street to deliver a case of beer to former Governor Al Smith in his office at the Empire State Building. (Smith was a tireless opponent of Prohibition.)

Next, the Clydesdales toured New England and the Middle Atlantic states. While in Washington, D.C., the hitch delivered a case of beer to President Franklin Roosevelt at the White House. And so an advertising icon was born—and lives on to this day. The Budweiser Clydesdales continue to serve as the international symbol of Anheuser-Busch.

Today, the company owns about 250 of the horses. To qualify for one of the hitches, a Budweiser Clydesdale must be:

- a gelding
- at least four years old
- eighteen hands (6 feet) high
- between 2,000 and 2,300 pounds
- bay in color with a blaze of white on the face, a black mane and tail, and long white hair called "feathers" on all four legs and feet

And what big feet those are!

Clydesdales' horseshoes measure more than twenty inches (from end to end) and each weighs about five pounds. Typically, a shoe worn by a riding horse weighs about one pound and is half as long as that of a Clydesdale. Like the shoes, the harness and collar (which together weigh about 130 pounds) are individually fitted for each animal.

Each Budweiser Clydesdale team consists of ten horses; eight for the hitch and two alternates. The horses are posi-

Courtesy of Anheuser-Busch Companies

tioned in the hitch according to physical ability. The pair in front typically is the fastest and most agile. Horses closest to the wagon (wheel horses) must be strong enough to start the wagon's movement and to use their weight to help slow or stop the vehicle.

Each horse typically eats between twenty and thirty-five quarts of whole grains and fifty to sixty pounds of hay each day. A Clydesdale drinks about thirty gallons of water each day.

Several Budweiser Clydesdales reside at the Anheuser-Busch brewery in St. Louis, in a beautiful brick stable with stained glass windows, built in 1885 on the grounds of the brewery. Other teams live in Menifee, California; San Diego, California; Merrimack, New Hampshire; and San Antonio, Texas. Clydesdales also are housed at Grant's Farm, the 281-acre ancestral home of the Busch family, in suburban St. Louis.

Members of the Griesedieck family, from left, are Henry L. Griesedieck and his sons, Anton, Henry E., Raymond, and Robert. Courtesy of Griesedieck Brothers Brewing Corporation.

In 1911, Anton Griesedieck's son, Henry, bought the Consumer's Brewery at Shenandoah and Lemp and named it the Griesedieck Brothers Brewery Company in honor of his sons: Anton, Henry, Raymond, Robert, and Edward. The company grew quickly, and just prior to Prohibition, Griesedieck Brothers Brewery was said to be first in local sales.

PROHIBITION CHANGES EVERYTHING

Prohibition, of course, changed everything. In 1918, President Woodrow Wilson signed the bill that went into effect January 16, 1920, outlawing alcoholic beverages across the land. During Prohibition, Griesedieck Brothers Brewery closed. The Lemp Western Brewery went under in 1922, after selling their Falstaff brand to brewer Joseph Griesedieck. (He later changed the corporate name to the Falstaff Corporation.)

Anheuser-Busch responded to Prohibition primarily by diversifying. During the thirteen dry years, the company sold malt syrup, corn syrup, and baker's yeast; began manufacturing refrigerated trucks; and marketed soft drinks, including one called Bevo that was reminiscent of the tart taste of beer. Finally, on April 7, 1933, beer was declared legal in the nation once more.

Anheuser-Busch and Falstaff were up and running quickly. By summer, Griesedieck Brothers Brewery was once again in operation as well. Under the guidance of Joseph Griesedieck's offspring, Falstaff transformed into a large regional brewery. Henry Griesedieck's heirs at Griesedieck Brothers Brewery concentrated on the St. Louis market and earned a big following by sponsoring radio broadcasts of Cardinals baseball games. (That ended when Anheuser-Busch acquired the team in 1953.)

Historians note that the Western Brewery in Belleville showed some muscle in the late 1940s and 1950s, when their Stag beer was said to be the largest seller in the metropolitan area. At the time, the Western Brewery belonged to a branch of the Griesedieck

Courtesy of Mid-America Grocers Association

family, which bought the brewery in 1912. (For years, the Griesediecks, the Lemps, and the Busches all had business interests, sometimes as silent partners and sometimes in legal disputes, with breweries in Illinois, most notably in Belleville and East St. Louis.)

In the late 1940s, Western advertised Stag as "brewed with Golden Quality since 1851," though the beer was originally brewed under another name. Originally established in the late 1850s, Western Brewery's signature product for a long time was Kaiser beer. When the name became a detriment (think Kaiser Wilhelm II of Germany), the brewery held a contest to rename the beer. George E. Wuller suggested Stag and won twenty-five dollars in gold for his trouble.

In the late 1950s, the Griesedieck Western Brewery was sold to the Carling Brewing Company of Cleveland, Ohio. Stag beer continued to be produced in Belleville for years, even after Carling sold the brewery in 1979 to another firm. The last Belleville-based bottle of Stag beer was produced in 1988, when the brewery closed. Elsewhere, the Griesedieck cousins at Falstaff bought out the cousins at Griesedieck Brothers Brewery in 1957. When Falstaff's brewery operations in St. Louis closed in 1977, Anheuser-Busch was the only game in town.

Today, Anheuser-Busch has more than one hundred brands. Budweiser, which was introduced in 1876, and Bud Light, first produced in 1982, are the two top-selling beers in the world.

JUST THE TICKET!

THE BREWERY SCENE TODAY

In 1991, Tom Schlafly and Dan Kopman opened the first new brewery in St. Louis in over fifty years. Today, their Saint Louis Brewery, at 2100 Locust Street, produces "a wide range of traditional beers that pay tribute to the area's great history," and the adjoining brewpub, the Tap Room, is a lively spot for lunch or dinner. ("It's more fun to eat in a bar than to drink in a restaurant," says Schlafly.)

The business grew gradually. In 1993, the Saint Louis Brewery got its first draft account: Blueberry Hill. By 1996, the company was selling its Pale Ale and Oatmeal Stout in bottles. A year later, they were selling beer at Busch Stadium. In 1999, the brewery held the first HOP in the City, an annual beer festival where revelers could sample Saint Louis Brewery products. In 2003, Schlafly Bottleworks opened in Maplewood, followed by a restaurant on the premises one year later.

"The most important thing I've learned is that the best sociologists in the world are in the hospitality business," says Schlafly. "If you're a professor, and you're wrong, you still get a paycheck. If you guess wrong in the hospitality industry, you're out of business."

Tom Schlafly is very much in business. In addition to brewing more than forty craft beers, the Saint Louis Brewery sponsors Robert Burns Night, an Oyster Festival, and an annual art show called Art Outside that features local artists and local beers. "In my book," says Schlafly, "our business is much more like jazz than a symphony—we've been improvisational since we started."

A couple of things didn't work out—serving breakfast, for instance, or a short-lived coffeehouse. Two other moves, though, hit the high notes: Brew masters James Ottolini (at the Bottleworks) and Stephen Hale (at the Tap Room). Ottolini, who studied French,

TOM SCHLAFLY: ON BEER DRINKERS

Tom Schlafly, the founder and owner of the Saint Louis Brewery, identifies three types of beer drinkers in St. Louis:

- The Anheuser-Busch loyalist who drinks only Anheuser-Busch products
- The craft beer aficionado "who never sullies his (or her) palate with mainstream beer"
- The crossover drinker who keeps Bud Light in the refrigerator at home but wants something different when out to dinner

"For us, the third is the most important. If people want a change of pace, we're there," says Schlafly.

"Beer is as varied and complex as wine, but we don't want to make the mistake that some wineries made—making what you sell unapproachable for consumers. We don't want people to be afraid to order, or feel like they don't know the vocabulary."

He adds, "Fortunately for us, people in this town have a huge amount of interest in beer."

"When we opened in 1991, there was a lot of skepticism," Schlafly recalls. "We were one of the first in the craft beer business in St. Louis, and a lot of people thought it would be difficult for us to open because of Anheuser-Busch. There is a tremendous loyalty in this town to Anheuser-Busch, and most St. Louisans can name the CEOs there. In fact, Anheuser-Busch is so institutionalized, it's called 'The Brewery.'"

"We're never going to have brand loyalists to the same extent that Anheuser-Busch, Miller, and Coors do," he adds. "Our customers are tasters. But I like to think we have extended the palate of beer drinkers."

Courtesy of Saint Louis Brewing Company

also knows how to belly dance. And Hale, Schlafly says, was a classics major in college and has previously worked as a sea urchin diver and a chimney sweep.

Something else worked for Schlafly, too. He tells his success story in his book, *A New Religion in Mecca: Memoir of a Renegade Brewery in St. Louis.*

Several other brewers make craft beers in the metropolitan area. Founded in 2000 by Fran and Tony Caradonna, the O'Fallon Brewery at 26 West Industrial Drive in O'Fallon, Missouri, makes three "everyday" beers, a draft beer called O'Fallon 5-Day IPA, and several seasonal beers. O'Fallon is a manufacturing brewery that does not sell directly to customers.

The Augusta Brewing Company operates a microbrewery and beer garden in Augusta as well as Square One Brewery at 1727 Park Avenue in Lafayette Square, which offers "micro bites" and "macro bites."

Other local microbreweries that operate in conjunction with brewpubs include:

- Wm. D. Alandale Brewing Company, 105 East Jefferson Avenue in Kirkwood
- Buffalo Brewing Company, 3100 Olive in midtown
- Granite City Food & Brewery, 11411 Olive Boulevard in Creve Coeur
- Morgan Street Brewery, 721 North Second Street on Laclede's Landing
- Trailhead Brewing Company, 921 South Riverside, St. Charles

You say beer is not your beverage of choice? Read on…

MISSOURI'S WINERIES

At the beginning of 2008, Missouri was home to seventy-six wineries—big wineries, small wineries, and wineries in between. Collectively, estimated sales for 2007 surpassed 352,000 cases of wine. These vineyards covered some 1,400 acres across the state, and the industry provided full-time jobs for more than 6,000 people.

Here's just how rosé . . . er, rosy the picture is, and this is in spite of the killing freeze that did so much damage in the spring of 2007: The economic impact of wine and grapes on Missouri's economy for 2007 was estimated at $701.2 million.

That's a lot of money!

"Yes, that is a lot of money," says Jim Anderson, executive director of the Missouri Wine & Grape Board, which is part of the Department of Agriculture. "Missouri ranks about tenth in annual wine production, and we're glad to see this growing diversification in Missouri agriculture."

Anderson, based in Jefferson City, also serves as chairman of the State Associations Council for Wine America, and he says that as Missouri goes, so goes the nation. "Ten years ago, there were 2,000 wineries in America, and today there are over 5,000. Grapes are now the sixth largest crop in the country—we've got grapes growing in forty-four states and wineries in all fifty."

A few more wineries are expected to open here in the course of 2008, and that's more good news. "New wineries, new faces—that always brings so much more to an area, including bed and breakfast places, restaurants, and shops," says Anderson.

Founded in 1855, Adam Puchta Winery in Hermann is the oldest continuously owned farm and family winery in Missouri, and it is said to be one of a handful of wineries established well before Prohibition that are still standing in the United States.

St. James Winery in St. James is the largest winery in the state, producing more than 300,000 gallons of wine a year. Seventy percent of the state's wineries are small producers, making less than 5,000 gallons each, or about 2,100 cases per year. Claverach Farm and Vineyards in Eureka is the smallest, farming just seven acres and specializing in wines bottled "with minimal filtration or other intervention."

As everyone who lives here knows, Missouri specializes in all kinds of weather—freezing cold, searing heat, and everything in between, sometimes all on the same day. We experience gentle rains, tornado-force winds, hailstorms, and that personal favorite, "a wintry mix" of rain, sleet, and ice.

Grapes grow in a vineyard at Stone Hill Winery in Hermann. Courtesy of Missouri Wine & Grape Board.

Which wine grapes will put up with Missouri weather? The following:

- Catawba
- Cayuga White
- Chambourcin
- Chardonel
- Concord
- Norton/Cynthiana
- St. Vincent
- Seyval blanc
- Traminette
- Vidal blanc
- Vignoles

MISSOURI WINE COUNTRY TIMELINE

The Missouri Wine & Grape Board has compiled a timeline of our state's wine industry, and with their permission, we reprint that history (slightly edited) here.

1837: German settlers establish the town of Hermann on the banks of the Missouri River. Although too rocky for many crops, the ground around Hermann is well suited to growing wine grapes. A decade later, Hermann's wineries are producing over 10,000 gallons of wine a year. Eventually more than sixty wineries populate the small town, and by the 1880s, wine lovers in America and Europe are enjoying two million gallons of Missouri wine each year.

1870s: A dangerous vineyard pest, the phylloxera louse, destroys enormous tracts of vineyards in France. Missouri helps rebuild the European vineyards by sending phylloxera-resistant American rootstock to be grafted with French vine cuttings. The resultant vines prove extremely hardy and soon the French wine industry is back on its feet.

Late 1800s: Italian immigrants establish vineyards in the St. James area of Missouri. The state's wine industry thrives at the turn of the century, with about one hundred wineries operating throughout the state.

1920: Prohibition deals a near-fatal blow to the Missouri wine industry. When the 18th Amendment is repealed thirteen years later, little remains of the once strong industry. Only St. Stanislaus Novitiate in St. Louis survives, where Jesuits make sacramental wines throughout Prohibition. Negative after-effects

JAKE HAFNER: WINNING US OVER WITH NEW WINES

Courtesy of Monica Giardina

Jake Hafner, the proprietor of 33 Wine Shop and Tasting Bar in Lafayette Square, does not remember his first glass of good wine, but he remembers when he decided to get out of the kitchen and work with people.

"I was in New York, studying at the French Culinary Institute, when I realized I was more a front-of-the-house kind of guy," recalls Hafner. "That was around the same time I started taking additional wine classes—and now here I am."

A native St. Louisan, Hafner opened 33 in February 2001, when he was just twenty-six. "I would have needed more money and would have had to be older to do this in New York," he says. "Besides, I really like this neighborhood—it felt like a natural fit for the business."

The 33 Wine Shop and Tasting Bar, named for the year Prohibition was repealed, is located at 1913 Park Avenue.

Hafner carries between 750 and 800 wines from all over the world. "My vision is to operate a family-owned business that promotes smaller winemakers who make great products but who maybe don't have the money to market those products," he says. "I don't cater to anything mass market."

So if you pop into 33, rather than ask for a glass of the wine or beer (Hafner has about eighty different beers) that you usually have or what you had last time you were in—consider asking what Hafner recommends that particular day, what just arrived, or what he can't wait to pour for you.

As Hafner sees it, that's his job. "If I provide the comfortable, easy choices, if I encourage customers to follow the path of least resistance, then how will anyone experience that special moment of awakening to something new?"

ANTHONY BOMMARITO: A LOOK BACK—AND AHEAD

"I got in this business at the right time, when people were beginning to learn about and appreciate better wines," says Anthony Bommarito, who founded A. Bommarito Wines in 1991. "At the time, Missouri was not only lagging behind the East and West Coast markets in the quality of wine, but the Midwest was kind of a dumping ground for older vintages."

Bommarito opened the first temperature-controlled warehouse in the state and watched as other distributors followed suit. He sought out small wineries making quality products, winemakers who grow their own grapes or make their own wine—preferably both—and then watched as his competitors also elevated their standards.

Today, with offices in St. Louis and in Kansas City, A. Bommarito Wines is the largest wine distributor in Missouri. The warehouse at 2827 South Brentwood Boulevard stocks between five and six hundred different wines from all over the world.

"I feel good that we have raised the level of interest in fine wines and helped improve the quality of life in this state," says Bommarito.

Bommarito notes that in the fine dining business, restaurant owners always have offered wine with dinner, but outside that realm, for a long time drinking wine was not the norm. "Today, wine isn't saved for special occasions," he notes. "Today, wine relates to all kinds of food—steak, pizza, or a hamburger."

Pizza? Hamburger? For the record, Bommarito recommends a Sangiovese with pizza and Zinfandel with a hamburger. "Zinfandel is an American wine," he says. "Why not drink it with an American meal?"

Here are some additional tips from Bommarito:

- Trust your own palate. "Don't rely on somebody to tell you what's the best," he says. "Be confident—if you like it, drink it."

- Be wary of the phrase "the best cheap wine." Bommarito contends that "best" and "cheap" are not words that belong together. Instead, seek out quality wines offered at fair prices.

- If you can afford a ten-dollar bottle of wine, buy that. If you can afford to spend forty or sixty dollars, do so. "It's no different than when you could afford this tie or that suit or where you could afford to rent at first," says Bommarito.

Courtesy of Anthony Bommarito

"Go up a step each time that you can."

- Don't be afraid to taste different wines. "If you are buying a case of wine, don't buy all the same wine," he says. "Mix it up."

What lies ahead for the wine business?

"I don't think we'll see many new varietals, because every region in every country seems to be almost fully explored," says Bommarito. "I do think the technology will continue to improve and that we will continue to see better quality wines coming from every country."

of Prohibition in the form of high liquor taxes and license fees linger for decades, preventing the Missouri wine industry from reestablishing itself.

1960s and 1970s: The rebirth of the commercial wine industry in Missouri begins with the restoration of several original wineries. The early pioneers work hard to regain the former stature of the wine industry amid a slowly changing cultural and regulatory environment.

1980: Augusta becomes the first federally recognized American Viticultural Area (AVA). (The wine regions around Hermann, the southwest Missouri Ozark Mountains and highlands, and the south central region around St. James also have been designated as AVAs.)

Also in 1980, the Missouri Wine Advisory Board is formed, and a new tax on wine subsequently enables the establishment of the Missouri Wine & Grape program. A state viticulturalist is hired to assist in the restoration process and universities here begin working with winemakers to determine grape varieties suitable for Missouri's climate.

2000s: The Missouri wine industry in the new millennium is thriving. The number of wineries jumps to more than sixty-five and Missouri wineries produce diverse, complex, and sophisticated wines, wines that easily earn top awards in national and international competitions.

2003: Missouri legislators designate Norton/Cynthiana as the official state grape.

2005: The Missouri Wine & Grape Board is formed. The board directs funds from a state-wide tax on wine sales for research, education and marketing of the Missouri wine industry.

2006: Funded by the Missouri Wine & Grape Board, the Institute for Continental Climate Viticulture and Enology is established at the University of Missouri in the College of Agriculture, Foods, and Natural Resources. The institute conducts research on grape varieties and vineyard management techniques that contribute to the growth of the wine industry in Missouri and the Midwest.

Areas of research at the institute include:

• Cultural practices for Missouri soils and climate

• Development of disease-resistant and high-yield grape varieties

• Insect and other pest controls

• Rootstock development

• Fermentation and wine production

• Storage, handling, and service in the wine industry

The institute also is considering developing a statewide grape breeding program and developing new grape varieties that will take kindly to Missouri's eclectic weather.

What does the future hold? More wines, better wines, and continued growth of Missouri's wine industry!

Hermanhoff Winery. Courtesy of Missouri Wine & Grape Board.

LUCIAN DRESSEL: MOVING THE WINE BUSINESS FORWARD

In February of 1981, California's Napa Valley was named the second American Viticultural Area, a federal designation of a wine district.

Where was the first? Augusta, Missouri, so named in June of 1980.

Lucian Dressel (along with Clayton Byers and Howard Nason) was responsible for the designation in Augusta. At the time, Dressel owned Mount Pleasant Winery, about an hour's drive from downtown St. Louis.

Today, Dressel is the general manager and winemaker at Mary Michelle Winery in Carrollton, Illinois, about one hour northwest of St. Louis. There, his goal is to produce "an affordable world-class wine from Illinois-grown grapes." He also is busy breeding new grapes—crossing Norton grapes (also known as Cynthiana) with Zinfandel and also with Cabernet Sauvignon grapes.

The idea, says Dressel, is to combine the flavor components of Cabernet and the hearty qualities of Norton. "The Norton is disease- and winter-resistant, and it makes a neutral wine, so it's ideal as a breeding grape," says Dressel. "Besides, any grape that's half Cabernet has to be better than a grape that is not."

Breeding grapes is a new frontier for Dressel. "I got into this by accident," he says. Once the owner of milk, cheese, and ice cream–processing companies,

Dressel and his family bought Mount Pleasant Winery in 1966. By 1969, he had bottled his first wines. He has won gold medals for wine in all the major national contests, and a gold medal for Port awarded at the British House of Commons. In 1993, Dressel sold the winery and moved to Davis, California.

"I lived a few miles from a huge vineyard with lots of varieties," Dressel recalls. "I had a small vineyard in my side yard, and I put in some Cabernet, Zinfandel, and Norton, and got started in grape breeding."

Grape breeding, it turns out, is an intensive project limited to ten days each spring. "Grapes are flowering plants, and the flower has an intense smell to it—something like dime store perfume," says Dressel. Worse, Dressel is allergic to grape flowers. Still, he prevails.

Dressel's efforts at Mary Michelle are "rolling along." The vines are for sale, and he is working with growers in ten states. "We're past the cultivation stage. The grape tastes like both Norton and Cabernet, but it is a new grape that has its own flavor profiles. At this point, we've got to put what we have in a wine vat and see how it does."

In 2009, Dressel hopes to produce twenty barrels from the new grapes, which he will age in different woods. His expectations are high. "Within fifty years, these grapes will replace all the grapes now grown in the eastern United States." he says. Dressel pauses and laughs. "Of course, I won't be here to see if that actually happens."

TONY KOOYUMJIAN: MISSOURI'S "SWEET" WINE HISTORY

"Older people think of sweet wine when they think of Missouri," says Tony Kooyumjian, "and there is a reason for that." Kooyumjian, who owns Augusta Winery and Montelle Winery, explains it this way: "In the early 1800s, Missouri was second in the country in wine production. During Prohibition, all the wine grapes were pulled out of the ground, but a lot of farmers here kept growing Catawba, Niagara, and Concord grapes, which all were used to make grape juice and grape jelly."

After Prohibition, vineyard owners made wine out of the only grapes they had—the juice grapes. These grapes, says Kooyumjian, all had "distinct, hard-hitting flavors," but they did not have the finesse of wine grapes.

"Wines produced from the juice grapes had a lot of bitterness from the aggressive tannins. To balance that out, the winemakers produced them sweet, and that set the tone," he says. "And that's how Missouri wine drinkers acquired a taste for sweetness—but also for foxy flavors and aromas."

End of story?

Hardly. Today, Missouri wines are made from wine grapes, and experimentation has led winemakers in the state to identify wine grapes that do well in our climate and also make worthy wines.

"In the twenty-seven years I've been in this business, we're only working with two varieties now that we started out

with—the Seyval Blanc and Vidal Blanc," says Kooyumjian. "All the others are new—and today, half the wine we sell at Augusta and Montelle is dry."

Augusta Winery's 2004 Chambourcin (a dry red wine) was the winner of the 2007 Governor's Cup, awarded for the best Missouri wine. Kooyumjian's 2003 Norton (another dry red wine) took the gold medal and was named Best of Class in the same competition. Some of his other wines have won Best of Show in several competitions in California, and the German wine magazine *Selection* named Augusta Winery's 2001 Chardonel as "Best U.S.A. Wine." The runner-up? Montelle Winery's 2001 Dry Vignoles.

Overall, how do Missouri's wines rate? Kooyumjian is ready with his answer: "I've always said that a well-made wine, regardless of the grapes—a wine with fragrance, finish, and tannins in balance—will be a pleasing wine."

WATERING HOLES

You're nursing a beer, sipping a dirty martini, throwing back shots. You're at your favorite bar, and you're thinking about everything except how all this got started, right?

Listen up: Legend has it that the first tavern in what is now the United States opened in Boston in—wait for it—1634. Of course, a "tavern" at that time was also a place for travelers to have a meal and rest before continuing on their journey. But the locals had a different goal when they set off for a nearby saloon.

That means you're part of a tradition that dates back almost 375 years, a time-honored tradition of stopping off for an alcoholic libation in the company of other jovial imbibers. Fun, huh?

In 1804, St. Louis boasted a bakery, two taverns, three blacksmiths, two mills, and a physician. The late Homer Bassford, a prolific journalist writing in the 1930s, reports that, originally, there was no licensing system in St. Louis for would-be tavern owners. Once the Louisiana Territory was officially transferred to the United States in 1804, a license fee of twenty-five dollars was established. During cool weather months, the fee could be paid in dressed deer skins. During hot weather, only cash was accepted.

Whiskey was also used as currency—records show that a man bought 640 acres "in the country" just southwest of St. Louis for 640 gallons of whiskey. The country was closer in then—land west of Tenth Street was all open fields, and many residents of what was known as "the village" were of the opinion that the city itself was full of "ruffians, robbers, swearers and swindlers."

According to Bassford, the first licensed tavern keepers in St. Louis were Emilien Yousti, Andre Andreville, and William Sullivan. Each opened a tavern with adjacent stables. Early taverns were not fancy places. Doors and windows had no screens, crude stoves provided little heat in winter, and more often than not, food was placed directly on the tables. Even good wine was served in unwashed goblets.

WELL-LUBRICATED CONSTITUTIONAL CONVENTION

Guess where some of our forefathers gathered in 1820 to draw up the first constitution for the state of Missouri?

In a bar—at the Missouri Hotel, on First Street in today's Laclede's Landing, to be exact. A report in the February 27, 1933, edition of the *St. Louis Star Times* newspaper notes that during

Built in 1818 on Wharf and Chestnut Streets as a fur warehouse, the Old Rock House later gained fame as a tavern. The current incarnation is at 1200 South Seventh Street. Courtesy of the Library of Congress.

the constitutional convention, the fellows "drank to each others' health—more than once."

The hotel's biggest competition at the time was the nearby Mansion House Hotel, which originally was a private home. A new owner added a big dining room and public meeting rooms, and opened for business. The two were considered "the chief taverns of the village in that day," and the rivalry was fierce, as each tried to outdo the other by serving the best whiskey and wine and playing host for the liveliest discussions.

At the time, saloons were considered reputable places, establishments where men could mix business with pleasure while enjoying refreshment—with no women present. On warm days, more than one judge was said to adjourn court to a nearby tavern in the middle of a trial, so participants could whet their respective whistles before getting back to work.

In his book *Taverns & Travelers*, Paton Yoder writes that in the mid-1820s hotels in St. Louis often organized expeditions and helped outfit caravans heading west. Yoder also writes of one traveler in the 1830s who stopped in a tavern near St. Louis for a meal. He ordered wild goose and was dismayed to find "skunk parts" on the plate.

Drivers deliver Budweiser beer soon after Prohibition. Courtesy of Mid-America Grocers Association.

Crowds in these early watering holes were not necessarily well behaved. In 1842, Charles Dickens stayed at the Planters House Hotel in downtown St. Louis, and his report on the bar there included observations of men "bragging about hunting, tussling with Indians and bears." Customers included people speaking "many dialects—French, Spanish, Irish, some southerners, and the occasional Yankee."

In those days, "public houses" served wine, beer, and spirits, while grocers sold whiskey from barrels. In 1894, J. D. Fehrmann opened shop at 1111 North Second Street. An article published in the *St. Louis Globe-Democrat* on December 2, 1962, reported that Fehrmann sold whiskey jugs to farmers and then encouraged them to fill up the jugs in his "Sample Room."

In 1903, George Himmler opened the Geyer House at Broadway and Geyer. The bar's claim to fame was a log cabin built over the bar. An ornamental coal stove was the main attraction at the Derby Bar at Twelfth and Pine. A photo from 1912 shows the owners, brothers Bert and Joe Brabazon, surrounded by men wearing suits and ties, all grimly clutching bottles of beer. Julius Vogel's Sugarhouse Exchange, at First and Biddle, was another longtime landmark saloon.

PRIOR TO PROHIBITION

Newspaper accounts report that in the Gay Nineties and beyond, a few signature bars in St. Louis—many of them located in restaurants—were "known the world over for the excellence of their vintages." Delmonico's at Lindell and Taylor was considered "an elegant roadhouse for champagne nightcaps," and the Morgan Club at Jefferson and Chestnut also was a popular nightspot. The Woodlawn Grove—later known as Busch's Grove—opened in 1890 at what is now 9160 Clayton Road, attracting city folk who arrived in horse-drawn carriages to drink and dine.

At the time, many bars were open twenty-four hours a day, seven days a week. Bloeser's at 418 Olive did a brisk business on Sunday mornings, as cocktails at that time of day "were a weekly rite for men." Proprietor John Bloeser was said to have invented the gin rickey, named for a well-known politician who downed the drink each morning "as his morning bracer."

Other popular bars of the day included Phil Hellery's, across from the Merchant Exchange, where every drink cost five cents; Lippe's, where "serious drinkers played a matinee engagement"; Bart Readey's place in the Commercial Building, which featured a "long dry punch served in a vase"; and John Howard's at Leffingwell and Olive, where the "West End aristocrats" drank.

The shadow that hung over the Gay Nineties was the knowledge that "religiously motivated women" all over the country were busy working to close down the liquor industry, and with it, the saloons, which they considered vile—rife with prostitution, gambling, and underage drinking. In his book *A History of Anheuser-Busch, 1852–1933*, Ronald Jan Plavchan reports that in many states the "drys" had managed to pass "high-license laws that required saloonkeepers to pay $500 or $1,000 annually to operate their businesses within the state."

Dancers cluster on stage at the Gilded Cage in Gaslight Square in this photo taken October 1, 1965, by Edward Goldberger. Courtesy of Missouri History Museum, St. Louis.

Most bar owners couldn't afford that fee, so they approached the larger breweries for help. In many cases, the brewers chose to buy the lot and the building, pay the license fee, and then rent the bar back to the former owner. "This practice of owning saloons in order to promote one's beers became universal among brewers," writes Plavchan. "In the City of St. Louis, for example, the brewers owned about sixty-five percent of the city's saloons."

One of those saloons was at 6715 Manchester Avenue. The Failoni family bought the bar in 1916 from the Lemp Brewing Company. Legend—or maybe it's only rumor—has it that Failoni's operated as a speakeasy during Prohibition. Today, the family-owned place is still popular, with a friendly atmosphere that draws in customers from all over.

All the imbibing came to a halt (all the legal imbibing, anyway) on January 16, 1920, when Prohibition went into effect. The 18th Amendment to the Constitution prohibited the manufacture, sale, and transportation of intoxicating beverages throughout the nation. And "intoxicating beverage" was defined as "any beverage containing more than one-half of one percent of alcohol by volume."

That said, here's what really happened: "The American people took to drinking on a scale never before known or believed possible," writes Roland Krebs in his book *Making Friends Is Our Business: 100 Years of Anheuser-Busch*. "The hip flask became as common as the match book."

ROOSEVELT TO THE RESCUE

The so-called dry spell lasted thirteen long years. At President Franklin D. Roosevelt's urging, Congress first modified the legal definition of an intoxicating beverage. On April 7, 1933, consuming "3.2 beer" became legal once again, and on December 5 of the same year, the 21st Amendment repealed Prohibition fully.

In the 1940s and 1950s, local bars flourished. On Friday nights, entire families headed for the neighborhood tavern. Fathers sat at the bar, drinking beer. Mothers sat at the tables, nursing Manhattans. Kids commandeered the booths, where they played Crazy Eights, Old Maid, and Go Fish while downing "mocktails" named for Shirley Temple or Roy Rogers, made from soft drinks mixed with maraschino cherry juice.

"As a kid in south St. Louis, I remember that every family had its own neighborhood bar," recalls Jack Parker, longtime owner of O'Connell's Irish Pub. "By the age of eighteen or so, you learned where you could go. I remember the Tyrolean Bar and Becker's at Grand and Bates. Garavelli's was at Grand and Olive. They had a stand-up bar and a pool hall upstairs. My father hung out there quite a bit." Parker also says that the original Culpepper's was a watering hole after World War II, located right where it is now, at 300 North Euclid.

O'Connell's, said to be the first Irish pub in town, opened in 1962 in the glittering entertainment district known as Gaslight Square, which got going in the mid-1950s. The boundaries of

the district stretched just a few blocks, from Pendleton east to Whittier, with most of the bars, clubs, and restaurants located along Olive or on Boyle. People came from all over the country to experience Gaslight Square. Some nights, say those in the know, the streets were so crowded that it could take thirty minutes to drive two blocks.

Big names performed in Gaslight Square, many of them at the Crystal Palace, owned by Jay and Fran Landesman. Among the top entertainers who came to town were Barbara Streisand, Miles Davis, Jackie Mason, Tom and Dick Smothers, George Carlin, and Lenny Bruce. To this day, Woody Allen talks about St. Louis as one of the first places he played clarinet publicly, sitting in with Singleton Palmer's band in between Allen's shows at the Crystal Palace. Phyllis Diller performed in Gaslight Square. She lived here, too, originally in an apartment above a drugstore at Shaw and Vandeventer and later in the heart of Webster Groves.

The glory days of Gaslight Square were over by 1967. O'Connell's was the last business to close, moving in 1972 to its current location at 4652 Shaw Boulevard, a building that dates back to 1905 and was once owned by Anheuser-Busch. "Probably, I should have gotten out sooner, but Gaslight Square was an interesting place, and it was an interesting time, politically," says Parker.

"I remember going with Sam Deitsch and Herbie Balaban to clubs on the north side, and Spider Burke was the first deejay to introduce jazz to a young white audience on the radio," says Parker. "I also remember stopping in at a few unlicensed watering holes where you would be served a coffee cup filled with booze."

The Crystal Palace in Gaslight Square printed some menu items on a fan. Courtesy of Jack Parker.

Irv Schankman captured the allure of Gaslight Square in this photo from 1964. Courtesy of Missouri History Museum, St. Louis.

JACK PARKER: ALLEN GINSBERG—AND THEN SOME

Jack Parker. Courtesy of Jack Parker.

One cold night in February, deep in the mid-1960s, business was slow at O'Connell's Irish Pub, then at 454 North Boyle Avenue in Gaslight Square. A total of twelve people had dropped in over a four-hour period. Then the door opened and in came Russell Durgin, a professor of English and drama at Country Day School.

He brought a friend—Allen Ginsberg.

Ginsberg (1926–1997), should you be unaware—and you shouldn't—was a man of many facets, among them an iconoclastic poet and activist. The Allen Ginsberg Trust defines him this way: "Spiritual seeker, founding member of a major literary movement, champion of human and civil rights, photographer and songwriter, political gadfly, teacher and co-founder of a poetics school."

"Durgin had befriended Ginsberg in New York a few years earlier," recalls Jack Parker, longtime owner of O'Connell's and proprietor of Jack Parker's Fine Art and Antiques, located above the tavern. "This was when the Bohemians were fading out in the Village, when City Lights Bookstore was big in San Francisco, when people were talking about Jack Kerouac's *On the Road*—all that was going on," says Parker.

"Ginsberg talked for a while about the old days in the Village. Then he sat down in front of the fireplace—we had a great fireplace—and took off his shoes. He sat in a lotus position, and he got out little bells, finger cymbals. And then—Allen Ginsberg recited from *Howl*." (The famous first line goes: "I saw the best minds of my generation destroyed by madness . . .")

Parker pauses, remembering. He smiles. "It was a wonderful evening."

No matter how much you want to have been there, you can't!

You can, however, sit and sip a Guinness at the current incarnation of O'Connell's, at 4652 Shaw Boulevard. The bar boasts much of the original woodwork and fixtures, including chandeliers made in England that once hung in the Belgian exhibition hall at the 1904 World's Fair.

Many of the Irish artifacts—posters, pictures, and such—came from Ireland, collected by the original owners of the bar, which opened in 1962. Jack Seltzer, Ray Gottfried, and Dick Draper built O'Connell's Irish Pub. "They did it for a lark, for the fun of owning their own bar," recalls Parker. "They were regular customers at the Gaslight Bar, and they decided they wanted to drink in their own place. There was nobody Irish involved."

As Parker remembers it, Seltzer connected with "a guy in Ireland named Malachy," a cousin of one Rita Ryan of St. Louis. "Malachy scouted for old pub stuff that was going out of style in Dublin. People there were redoing the pubs—they all wanted the look of a cocktail lounge."

That's how O'Connell's got all the authentic whiskey signs and what Parker calls "a great portrait of Maud Gonne." Parker is responsible for the collection of empty Tullamore Dew jugs. The mounted animal heads? Ray Gottfried shot them.

And one cold night in February, deep in the mid-1960s, a night when business was slow at O'Connell's Irish Pub—Allen Ginsberg was there . . .

Allen Ginsberg. Courtesy of the Allen Ginsberg Estate

TOM SAVIO: KEEPER OF THE BOCCE COURTS

You can get a beer or a bite to eat at Milo's Bocce Garden, or you can play bocce—sometimes in the company of a bridal party in full wedding-day regalia, a kindergarten class learning the rules, or a busload of senior citizens who have dropped by for a game.

"One Saturday afternoon, a wedding party showed up after the ceremony. The couple had met at Milo's," says Tom Savio, co-owner with Joe Vollmer. Milo's is at 5201 Wilson Avenue on the Hill. "A few minutes later, another wedding party showed up. We had two brides, two grooms, and everybody else, all playing bocce."

Bocce is the Italian version of lawn bowling, a sport said to date back to the days of the Roman Empire. Milo's has two bocce courts (the only public courts in the area) behind the tavern. Monday through Thursday, over fifty teams play in evening leagues. At other times, pick-up games are encouraged, and newcomers are always welcome. (All players must be twenty-one, or accompanied by an adult.)

Michael Ceriotti on Milo's bocce court. Courtesy of Matthew Heidenry.

In the bar, Savio and Vollmer display a relic from Milo's earlier days: A Plexiglas bubble that depicts a miniature Budweiser beer wagon pulled by miniature Clydesdales. The Anheuser-Busch brewery dubbed this advertising effort a "Clydesdale Spectacular."

"This tavern was built in 1904 by the brewery, one of many corner taverns with apartments upstairs that were built to sell Anheuser-Busch products exclusively," says Savio. "When the salesmen from the brewery would drop in, they'd flash wads of cash and buy a beer for everyone in the place."

To let everyone in the neighborhood know that drinks were on the house, the tavern owner would lean a broom, bristles up, against the front of the building.

"Some fellows would follow the salesmen around all day, from bar to bar," says Savio. "That's what the old-timers tell me."

In those days, the bar at 5201 Wilson was called Merlo's. When Savio bought it in 1975, it was known as Wil-Mar's, in honor of the tavern's location at the corner of Wilson and Marconi. He changed the name to Milo's. Vollmer and Savio put in the bocce courts in 1989.

Inside, customers can play darts, pinball, or foosball in a room dedicated to a more recent era that came to an end: The Wall. Signatures proudly fill the walls of the back room, made by patrons who took the challenge to imbibe one of three lists of six beverages in an evening.

Outside—even in winter (kudos to participants in the Polar Bear Tournament)—bocce rules.

BAR HOPPING THE EASY WAY

In 1980, Dan Brennan and Steve Weaver penned *Harry's St. Louis Guide to Taverns, Pubs, Saloons and Other Drinking Establishments*, a gleeful romp full of fun facts about local bars. For instance:

- The Missouri Bar and Grill at 701 North Tucker has been a hangout for newspaper reporters for almost seventy years

- Rigazzi's, at 4945 Daggett, has been serving frozen fish bowls full of beer since 1957

- Thurmer's, at 3159 Cherokee for some five decades, sponsored softball, baseball, bowling, basketball, and volleyball teams

- The now-defunct Rose's Bar & Grill opened at 1933 Edwards in 1910 and welcomed many a bocce player over the years

- O'Shea's (now Seamus McDaniel's) at 1208 Tamm Avenue is said to be the oldest Irish saloon in continuous operation in the United States

- Llywelyn's in the Central West End was named for the Prince of Wales

Speaking of Llywelyn's, the 2007 edition of *The Days & Nights of the Central West End* reports that Jack Brangle and Jon Dressel opened the Welsh pub in 1975. Dressel then opened his own Welsh pub in 1998—Dressel's—half a block away, at 419 North Euclid.

In August 2006, both pubs attracted the attention of *Ninnnau*, the North American Welsh Newspaper. (Published in Basking Ridge, New Jersey, *Ninnnau* is pronounced "nin-eye" and means "us" or "we also." So says the banner, anyway.) Reporter David Parry awarded both pubs points for serving Felinfoel, a Welsh ale. One of our town's Irish pubs also garnered kudos in 2007, when *Esquire* named John D. McGurk's Irish Pub at 1200 Russell Boulevard as one of the "Best Bars in America."

John D. McGurk's Irish Pub celebrates the wearing of the green every day. Courtesy of McGurk's.

MORE THAN ONE BEST

Readers of the *Riverfront Times* routinely honor Blueberry Hill for Best Jukebox, Best Beer Selection, Best Hamburger, and Best Neighborhood Bar. *Sauce Magazine* Readers' Choice Awards have gone to Blueberry Hill in the following categories:

- Best Casual Dining
- Best Place to Take Out-of-Towners
- Best American Cuisine
- Favorite Bar and Grill
- Favorite Place to Recommend
- Favorite Restaurant with Live Music

Joe and Linda Edwards opened Blueberry Hill in 1972, at 6504 Delmar in the University City Loop. They filled the bar with pop culture memorabilia celebrating Chuck Berry, the Simpsons, the Beatles, and Star Wars, among others. "The displays on Howdy Doody and Chuck Berry are the biggest displays in the country, and I'm partial to those," says Joe Edwards. "I also really like the Pee Wee Herman collection."

Something else that Blueberry Hill has that other bars don't have (besides regular appearances by Chuck Berry, of course) is window displays. Through the years, Linda Edwards has created such themes as "Trimming Santa's Tree," "Easter Bunny's Kitchen," and "Witches' Night Out," as well as tributes to Elvis Presley, Dr. Martin Luther King, Jr., and Superman. Her display on the Dionne Quintuplets was featured in *Newsweek*.

"People have gotten married in our display window," says Joe Edwards. "Tons of couples have met here, but one couple actually got married in the window, complete with a minister, ten or eleven years ago. Now they come in with their four kids every Valentine's Day, to celebrate their anniversary."

Edwards' other favorite thing at his bar is the annual dart tournament, held on Mother's Day weekend every year. The 2008 tournament was the thirty-sixth year, and offered $5,000 in prizes. Several hundred people were expected to attend. "We hold the record for the oldest pub dart tournament in North America," says Edwards. "And to think I got conned into it."

Conned?

"Yes—the first couple weeks I was open, a guy from the neighborhood came in and asked about a dart board. I said I didn't have one, and the guy asked if I wanted to borrow his."

Edwards said no.

"The next day, a different guy came in, ordered a beer, and asked where our dartboard was. The day after that, a woman

Chuck Berry plays a regular gig at Blueberry Hill—much to the delight of loyal fans. Courtesy of Joe Edwards.

came in and asked about a dartboard. Finally, the first guy came back. I knew he'd sent in those other people, but I went ahead and borrowed the dartboard."

Edwards pauses, then laughs. "I'll always be grateful."

Charlie Becker, eighty-three, is grateful for a life spent working at a job he loves. Becker, a bar owner for fifty years, owned Joe & Charlie's along with Joe Scopolite when the bar was in Gaslight Square and later when it was on Clayton Road near Brentwood Boulevard. Today, Becker owns Krueger's, at 7347 Forsyth.

"The bar business has been good to me," says Charlie Becker, seated outside Krueger's on a warm, sunny day. "I went into this business because I had no money. I was thirty-three and had to get a job. A friend, a fellow who was a bartender, suggested I open a tavern, which is the average guy's club. It was a good idea."

Becker recalls his first night in the business. "Right at midnight, when our license went into effect, everybody sitting in the Puppet Pub on Clayton Road left and came over to our place,"

Joe & Charlie's on Clayton Road was an iconic St. Louis bar. Courtesy of Krueger's.

JOE EDWARDS: ANYONE FOR ABSINTHE?

Today, Blueberry Hill is known far and wide for its vast selection of beers, but when Joe Edwards first opened the bar in 1972, he offered only two selections: Schlitz Light and Schlitz Dark. "I often wondered if the dark beer was the same as the light, with food coloring," Edwards muses. Even worse, his first six months in business, Edwards had just a 3.2 beer license.

But that was then. Today, Blueberry Hill, at 6504 Delmar Boulevard in the University City Loop, sells eighteen beers on tap and sixty bottled beers from all over the world, with "guest" beers and draft selections also available seasonally.

"Now, we're at a level where we will stay," Edwards says.

Most of his customers order beer, but Edwards has seen interest in mixed drinks increase, especially in the past ten years. Before that, he notes, typical requests were for a Seven and Seven (that's Seagram's 7 whiskey and 7-Up) or a Cuba Libre (rum and cola). "In the last ten years, people wanted to try single-malt scotches, then different bourbons—and in the past five years, what really took off were the vodkas."

What's next?

Edwards predicts new interest in upscale rums. "We've got one called Pyrate Rum that sells for thirty-five dollars a shot," he says. "It's the kind of thing you'd order when you really want to celebrate closing a deal or if you were showing off for a date."

What else? "Absinthe is now legal in the United States for the first time in ninety-five years," Edwards says. He sells the drink for nine dollars at his Flamingo Bowl (1117 Washington Avenue), said to be the first place outside New York City to carry it. Green in color, absinthe is an anise-flavored spirit distilled from wormwood.

"Wormwood has an ingredient in it said to cause hallucinations," Edwards says. "Supposedly, Van Gogh was tripping on absinthe when he cut off his ear." So far, so good—no severed ears cluttering up the bowling lanes.

Back at Blueberry Hill, what's the most popular drink at the bar? Edwards laughs. "Bud Light."

---

says Becker, a grin spreading across his face. "Those were the days when Jack Parker was making barbecue in the alley and selling it to local bars."

Becker and Scopolite had acquired the third liquor license granted for Gaslight Square. A few years later, when thirty-seven places in the neighborhood had licenses, they closed Joe & Charlie's. They moved first to a spot on Brentwood Boulevard and then settled in at 8040 Clayton Road in 1992. That bar closed ten years later.

In 1965, Becker bought Krueger's, a no-frills neighborhood bar where Becker's son Adam greets customers with a quick grin and a ready handshake. The sign on the mirror behind the bar reads: "This mirror is older than you are and it is clean." The menu features bar food (try the fried pickles) as well as salads and sandwiches, including the popular three-cheese grilled

sandwich from the old Joe & Charlie's.

Most of Becker's customers are people who have followed him from place to place through the years. "In this business, you have to like people, get to know people by name, but it's a good way to make a living," he says. "Today, little places like this are hard to find."

Asked how the bar business has changed in fifty years, Becker's response is short and to the point. "It hasn't," he says. "People go to bars to get out and have a good time. If they just wanted a beer, they would have one at home."

Watering holes, wineries, and breweries—we've got them all, either in the neighborhood or not too far from home. Let's raise a glass to them all, and be grateful it's legal.

Fresh Gatherings Café and Recipes

Fresh Gatherings Café of Saint Louis University's Doisy College of Health Sciences is a model for sustainable cuisine within an institutional environment. With the support of the Office of the Dean, the department of Nutrition and Dietetics has been operating the Fresh Gatherings Café since September 2004. The menus are developed from local and seasonal produce and livestock by culinary chefs who teach in the program. All of the farmers are within 150 miles of the campus in Missouri and Illinois, and most of them practice organic methods and are advocates of humane husbandry. The crops are all purchased at the peak of their freshness. Not only is the food delicious, but it is also healthy and nutrient dense.

In season, Fresh Gatherings Café serves vegetables grown in the department of Nutrition and Dietetics' own organic garden on the grounds of Saint Louis University. The department has a curricular thread in sustainable food systems, and the Fresh Gatherings Café provides a living classroom for many of our courses, as well as being a cornerstone for the culinary curriculum. Students leave the program and enter their careers with an appreciation of seasonal and sustainable cuisine.

The Fresh Gatherings Café is also a part of the "Gardens to Tables" USDA grant the department received and is nationally recognized as a pioneering enterprise in farm-to-cafeteria efforts and providing education and consultation to area programs including public school systems. The Gardens to Tables Consortium was formed to develop programs that increase the availability of nutritious food, provide sound nutrition education, increase physical activity, support sustainable food systems, and improve food preparation and preservation abilities among the families of Sigel,

Courtesy of Doisy College of Health Sciences

Maplewood-Richmond Heights, and L'Ouverture Schools. For seventeen years, SLU dietetic interns have been teaching lessons regarding the goals of the program involving the children in the garden growing fruits and vegetables at the schools.

The café is a leading program in sustainable food systems and recycling. The Fresh Gatherings Café uses compostable serviceware. The cups and straws are fabricated from corn, the plates are from sugar cane reed, and the utensils are from limestone. Food waste from the cafeteria goes back into the soil of the Saint Louis University garden for fertilization. The recycling plan is coordinated in collaboration with the Greenways Center of the Missouri Botanical Garden. Fresh Gatherings Café is a vendor at the Clayton Farmer's Market, and the department of Nutrition and Dietetics has initiated a garden market at Sigel Elementary, Maplewood-Richmond Heights, and L'Ouverture.

We are excited to share with you our favorite recipes from the Fresh Gatherings Café chefs. For more information, visit http://nd.slu.edu.

Courtesy of Doisy College of Health Sciences

Courtesy of Doisy College of Health Sciences

Recipes

Crimini Mushrooms Stuffed with Fresh Basil-Flavored Ricotta Cheese

From Mark E. Miller, certified executive chef and Saint Louis Chef of the Year, 2000.

1 (15-ounce container) part-skim ricotta cheese
3 ounces fresh basil
2 tablespoons fresh lemon juice
Salt and pepper
45 crimini mushrooms, skins removed and washed (Ozark Forest Mushrooms is a good source. See www.ozarkforest.com.)

Preheat oven to 375 degrees.

Place ricotta cheese and basil in a food processor or mixing bowl. Add lemon juice and seasoning to taste and mix until smooth. Using a piping bag or small spoon, place the ricotta mixture into the cavity of the mushroom.

Bake 5 to 8 minutes at 375 degrees. Serve immediately.

Note: This stuffing holds well in the refrigerator for future use if you don't use all the mushrooms.

Smoked Gouda and Caramelized Onion Stuffed Portobella Mushrooms

From Mark E. Miller.

1 medium Vidalia onion sliced thin (You may substitute another onion variety.)
Olive oil as needed
5 portobella mushrooms, 4 inches in diameter, cleaned and stems removed (Ozark Forest Mushrooms is a good source. See www.ozarkforest.com.)
7 ounces smoked Gouda, shredded on medium grate (Hautly brand smoked Gouda works best for this recipe.)
Salt and pepper

Preheat oven to 375 degrees.

Sauté onions over medium heat, stirring until they start to brown. Continue cooking, stirring until they are golden brown. Cool completely.

While the onions are cooling, lightly oil and season the clean mushrooms. Char grill or sauté the mushrooms over medium-high heat. Turn the mushrooms as they cook so they do not burn.

Mix the cooled onions with the grated smoked Gouda. Place the stuffing mixture into the stem sides of the mushrooms, making an even layer. Season to taste.

Bake at 375 degrees for 8 to 10 minutes, or until cheese melts. Let rest 2 to 4 minutes, slice like pizza, and enjoy.

Shredded Parmesan Tomato Bruschetta

From Mark E. Miller.

1 loaf crusty French bread, sliced in 25 to 30 (¼-inch thick) slices
Olive oil to brush on bread slices
1 pound diced roma tomatoes OR 1 (16-ounce) can diced tomatoes, drained
3 ounces basil pesto
1 tablespoon black pepper
1 tablespoon olive oil
6 ounces shredded Parmesan cheese

Preheat oven to 350 degrees.

Place sliced French bread on baking sheet. Brush with olive oil. Toast in oven until golden brown, approximately 4 to 5 minutes.

In a bowl, mix tomatoes, basil pesto, black pepper, and 1 tablespoon of olive oil. Place tomato mixture on French bread slices using a spoon or your hand, taking care to keep the mixture firmly attached to the bread. Top liberally with shredded Parmesan cheese, keeping the cheese on the bread as much as possible.

Bake at 350 degrees for 5 to 7 minutes. Serve immediately.

Yield: 25 to 30 bruschetta.

Note: Do not put mixture on bread more than 30 minutes before baking because the bread will become soggy.

Asian Noodle Salad

From Mark E. Miller.

For the dressing:
1 teaspoon fresh ginger, grated
1 teaspoon fresh garlic, minced
1 tablespoon soy sauce
1 teaspoon sesame oil
1 chili pepper
1 tablespoon sugar
$1/3$ cup rice wine vinegar
½ cup peanut oil
Salt and pepper to taste

For the salad:
2 pounds of Canton noodles (also known as Chinese Egg noodles)
½ pound snow peas, julienned
1 bunch scallions OR green onions, cut at an angle
1 tablespoon fresh coriander, minced
2 pounds shrimp, cooked, peeled and deveined

To make the dressing, combine ginger, garlic, soy sauce, sesame oil, chili pepper, sugar, rice wine vinegar, peanut oil, and salt and pepper. Let mixture sit at room temperature until ready to use.

To make the salad, cook the noodles as directed on the package.

In a large bowl, combine the noodles with the snow peas, scallions, coriander, and shrimp. Coat all, but do not saturate, with dressing. Reserve extra dressing to use before serving, as the noodles will absorb much of the dressing.

Roasted Veggie Pasta

From Mark E. Miller.

For the dressing:
Balsamic vinegar, to taste
Balsamic vinaigrette, to taste
Honey, to taste
2 teaspoons roasted red pepper paste to taste
2 teaspoons roasted garlic paste
1 teaspoon basil pesto

For the pasta:
2 roasted red, green and/or yellow peppers
2 roasted red and yellow onions
1 roasted yellow squash
1 roasted zucchini
4 large roasted tomatoes
½ cup roasted shiitake mushrooms
2 pounds pasta, cooked as directed
Fresh basil leaves, julienned

To make the dressing, combine balsamic vinegar, balsamic vinaigrette, honey, roasted red pepper paste, roasted garlic, and the basil pesto. Set dressing aside.

In a large bowl, combine peppers, onions, squash, zucchini, tomatoes, mushrooms, cooked pasta, and basil leaves. Add just enough dressing to coat but not saturate. If any dressing remains, save it to add later because the pasta always absorbs dressing.

Apple Cider Pumpernickel

From Todd Parkhurst, baking instructor.

(Note: Starters can be obtained from a local sourdough bakery, online at www.kingarthurflour.com, or at Fresh Gatherings in the Allied Health Building on Saint Louis University's South Campus. Once you have the starters, all you need to do is feed them with flour and water and you are on your way. The starters should be fully developed and have fermented at least 12 hours—or even overnight—since their last feed.)

1 cup water
¼ cup apple cider
2 ½ tablespoons sugar
2 tablespoons honey
4 teaspoons salt
1 ½ tablespoons Pomona's Apple Ambrosia (NOTE: Available at Blue Heron Orchards in Canton, Missouri.)
¾ cup rye starter
¾ cup whole wheat starter
1 1/8 cup medium rye flour
2 tablespoons dark cocoa powder
2 1/8 cups bread flour
1/3 cup plus 2 tablespoons whole wheat flour
¼ cup caraway seeds
¾ tablespoons instant yeast
1 ¼ cups golden raisins plumped in warm water and then drained
White flour
Corn meal for dusting the baking tray

In a large plastic tub, mix together the water, apple juice, sugar, honey, salt, and Apple Ambrosia. Stir in the rye starter and wheat starter.

Add the rye flour, cocoa powder, bread flour, whole wheat flour, caraway seeds, and yeast. Mix together until all the flour has been incorporated. Let stand for 25 to 30 minutes.

After resting the dough, place it in a five-quart bowl of an electric mixer (preferably a heavy duty model) and attach the dough hook. Mix on low speed for 20 minutes. Increase to medium speed and continue to mix for 8 to 10 minutes more.

Fold in the plumped raisins by hand until they are incorporated completely.

Transfer the dough to a plastic or glass tub or casserole dish that has been lightly sprayed with pan spray. Cover loosely with plastic wrap. (It's best if the wrap does not actually touch the dough.) Let the dough proof for 1 hour and 15 minutes at room temperature. (The dough should begin to develop some air holes at this point.)

Leaving the dough in the tub, fold one end of the dough over onto the other end of the dough and then flip it over so that the portion previously on the bottom is now on the top. Cover loosely again and let proof for another hour and 15 minutes.

After the dough has risen the second time, dump it out onto a floured work surface and divide the dough into two equal pieces. (The pieces should be approximately 1 ½ pounds each.) Gently roll each into a round loaf. Dip the top of the loaf into white flour, and deposit it into a linen lined proofing basket with the floured side of the loaf down and the bottom seam of the loaf up. (A roll basket lined with a lint-free tea towel works just as well.)

Cover each loaf loosely with plastic wrap and put into the refrigerator in an area that is running at about 42 to 45 degrees. The loaves will rise again very slowly. Best results are achieved if the dough is allowed to sit in the refrigerator for 30 to 40 hours before baking.

When you are ready to bake, preheat the oven to 375 degrees. To create steam in your oven, set an empty pan on the bottom shelf of the oven as it heats up to baking temperature. Pour some water on the hot pan when you put the loaves in to bake.)

Line a half-sheet pan with parchment paper and dust the paper with cornmeal so the loaves will not stick. Gently tip the loaves out of the baskets and onto the sheet pan. (Two loaves will fit on a half-sheet pan.) Score the top of the loaf with a sharp knife or razor to allow the loaf to expand while baking. Place pan in the center of the oven, create some steam with the bottom pan, and bake for 35 to 45 minutes, depending on the heat efficiency of your oven.

To test for doneness, thump the bottom of a loaf with your index or middle finger and listen for a hollow sound.

Yield: 2 (24-ounce) loaves.

Waldorf Salad

From Mark E. Miller.

For the dressing:
1 cup mayonnaise
¼ cup honey
¼ cup sugar
Cinnamon to taste

For the salad:
8 Granny Smith apples, diced large
8 Red Delicious applies, diced large
Sprite
Lemon juice
1 bunch celery, diced
2 cups toasted walnuts

To make the dressing, combine mayonnaise, honey, sugar, and cinnamon. Set aside.

To make the salad, soak the diced apples in a mixture of Sprite and lemon juice. Drain. Add the celery and the walnuts to the apples.

Toss with just enough dressing to coat, but not saturate.

Grilled Veggie Pesto Wrap

From Mark E. Miller.

5 yellow squash
5 zucchini
2 each green, red and yellow peppers
2 eggplants
6 large tomatoes
6 to 8 portobella mushrooms
4 red onions
Olive oil
Salt and pepper
Oregano
Basil
Thyme
Garlic powder
8 to 10 tortilla shells
Basil or tomato pesto mixed with a little mayonnaise
2 cups Asiago cheese

Slice all the vegetables about ¼ inch thick.

Rub with a mixture of olive oil, salt and pepper, oregano, basil, thyme, and garlic powder. Grill the vegetables and let them sweat and cool for 1 to 2 hours. After they are cooled, julienne the grilled vegetables.

Spread each tortilla shell with pesto and mayonnaise mixture. Pile the vegetables in the middle of each shell in an even row. Sprinkle with Asiago cheese. Roll the shell like a burrito.

Yield: 8 to 10 wraps.

About Doisy College of Health Sciences

Long a leader in health professions education, Saint Louis University began its first baccalaureate degree program in an allied health profession in 1929.

The Edward and Margaret Doisy College of Health Sciences was dedicated in 2001. The school was endowed by Margaret Doisy, widow of the 1943 Nobel laureate for physiology and medicine for his discovery of vitamin K.

Doisy College of Health Sciences includes the departments of Clinical Laboratory Science (including Cytotechnology), Health Informatics and Information Management, Medical Imaging & Radiation Therapeutics, Nutrition & Dietetics, Occupational Science & Occupational Therapy, Physical Therapy (including Athletic Training), and Physician Assistant Education. The college is an integral part of the Medical Center, home to Saint Louis University's schools of Medicine, Public Health, and Nursing and Saint Louis University Hospital. This location offers terrific outreach opportunities, an important part of the university's mission.

The Allied Health Building features modern, cutting-edge classroom and laboratory facilities that allow for interactive educational experiences:

- A state-of-the-art motion analysis lab for assessing gait, joint movements, and the forces related to them
- A food lab with six complete kitchenettes for teaching food science and basic food preparation
- A media and woodworking lab for analysis of routine activities of daily living
- A simulated medical office suite and exam rooms complete with videotaping capabilities and one-way mirrors for student observation

Dean Charlotte Royeen arrived at the Doisy College of Health Sciences in 2003.

About the Author

Patricia Corrigan loves to eat—and she likes writing about food as well. As restaurant critic for the *St. Louis Post-Dispatch*, she ate out on the paper's nickel for five years. Prior to that, she worked for five years as a food writer at the *Post*, happily interviewing hundreds of chefs, home cooks, restaurant owners, food manufacturers, and others in the food industry. She is the author of fifteen books, including *Bringing Science to Life: A Guide from the Saint Louis Science Center*; *Wild Things: Untold Tales from the First Century of the Saint Louis Zoo*; *The Extreme Earth: Waterfalls*; *Chemotherapy & Radiation for Dummies* (with Dr. Alan Lyss and Dr. Humberto Fagundes); and *Convertible Dreams.*

Courtesy of Wm Daniel File

Acknowledgments

How do you write a book about such a huge topic?

With help from many, many, enthusiastic people!

Some took me on tours of their businesses. Many made time for interviews, sent me needed written materials, or provided photos. Others made all these things possible. I am grateful for their help.

Among them are Tim Alexander, Josh Allen, Stanley Allen, Andy Ayers, Gena Bast, Reine Bayoc, Adam Becker, Charlie Becker, Pat Bergauer, Sinetsidk Berhanu, Hally Bini, Tom Birkenmeier, Keith Biver, Mark Bohnert, Anthony Bommarito, Vincent J. Bommarito, Joe Bonwich, Tim Brennan, Eric Brenner, Nancy L. Bridges, Troika Brodksy, Gunnar Brown, Tony Cannovo, Jack Carl, Gail Compton, Deb Connors, Lauren Crevits, Patricia J. Cummings, Ellen Cusumano, Gene Danekas, Dean Dittmar, Anthony Devoti, Kelly Donovan, Charlie Dooley, Lucian Dressel, Jen Duerfahrd, Karen Duffy, and Joanna Duley.

Also Maddie Earnest, Pat Eby, Jill Eckert-Tantillo, Joe Edwards, Jeff Fister, Richard Fister, Sam Hilmer, Mark Hitt, Patrick Horine, Clarence Hughes, Charles P. Gallagher Sr., Ramon Gallardo, Bill Greer, Ray Griesedieck, Sara Griffith, Bob Gunthner, Peter Hale, Paul and Wendy Hamilton, Joe Herrell, Marge and Ed Imo, Karrie Johnson, Mike Johnson, Adisa Kalkan, Mike Karandzieff, Bill Keaggy, Suzanne and Gus Koebbe, Dan Kopman, Tony Kooyumjian, Bebe Lichtenstein, Mike Lombardo, Paul A. Manno, Paul and Concetta Manno, Tim Mallett, Arlene Maminta, Mildred Mattfeldt-Beman, Lane McConnell, Andy Mehring, Orville Middendorf, Matthew Miller, Justin Minarick, Vita Moel, Ed Musen, and Eddie Neill.

Also Pat Newsham, Kathy Noelker, Barbara and Bill Olwig, Mina Overton, Jack Parker, Brett Palmier, Mike Parker, Lorenza Passeti, Richard Perry, Patty Pointer, Joe Pollack and Ann Lemons Pollack, Elaine and Ronnie Pratzel, Barb Ridenhour, Zoë Robinson, John Ruprecht, Harold D. Russell, Ron Ryan, Susan Ryan, Tom Savio, Tom

Schlafly, Mac Scott, Aaron Segall, Thom Sehnert, Dan Shaul, Paul Simon, Mayor Francis G. Slay, Francis R. Slay, Richard Stith, Trip Straub, Bobby Sweet, Michael Switzer, Michele Taylor, Darrell Thies, Dave Thies, Beth Thompson, Doug Travis, Bryan and Christina Truemper, J. Kim Tucci, Richard Ulrich, Beth von Behren, Jeff Watkin, Jim Weis, Andy Welle, Roslyn Wicks, Randy Wood, and Sandra Zak.

Some individuals cheerfully served as literary deputies, coming up with ideas and phone numbers for contacts, or providing moral support along the journey. Among them are Carolyn Bower, Jenny Bower, Bernice Brandmeier, Joan Bray, Dorothy Brinker, Jennifer Carns, Jim Creighton, Debbe Dalay, Betty Dameris, Karen Dameris, Judy Evans, Wm Daniel File, Chris French, Greg Gambero, Judy Guererro, Linda Gwyn, Ken Haller, Patricia Heidenry, Esther Katz, Susan Manlin Katzman, Doug King, Joel Krauska and Patricia Fox, Tom Krauska and Gerry Puglisi, Yue Ma, Ruth Mariam, Perrin McEwen, Kelly Mueller, Jim Nicholson, Carol North, Gail Pennington, Carol Porter, Beth Remming, Sanda Rosenblum, Karen Schneider, Helen Schrader, Chris and Hal Simpkin, Karen Sterbenz, Tina Telthorst, Nancy Tonkins, and Linda Walker.

On hand to help with research at the Missouri Historical Society Library Collections were Emily Jaycox, Dennie Northcott, and Ellen Thomasson.

Three talented and tenacious men—Matt Heidenry, Josh Stevens, and Bruce Burton—transformed my words into the book you now hold. Thanks, guys!

Now, let's go get something to eat!

Patricia Corrigan

Resources

General

Fresh Gatherings Café: http://nd.slu.edu
History: http://stlouis.missouri.org/neighborhoods/history/

Chapter 1: Restaurants

Websites
Agostino's: www.agostinoscatering.com/
Annie Gunn's: www.smokehousemarket.com/index.html
Araka: www.araka.com/
BARcelona Tapas: www.barcelonatapas.com/
Bevo Mill: www.bevomillstl.com/
Big Sky Café: www.allgreatrestaurants.com/page.
asp?id=6&name=Big%20Sky%20Cafe
The Blue Owl: www.theblueowl.com/
Blue Water Grill: www.allgreatrestaurants.com/page.
asp?id=5&name=Blue%20Water%20Grill
Boogaloo: www.boogaloostl.com/
Busch's Grove: www.buschsgrove.com
Caito's: www.caitosrestaurant.com/
Casa Gallaro: www.casagallardo.com
The Cedars: http://cedars.straymonds.net/
Charlie Gitto's: www.charliegittos.com/
Chevy's: www.chevys.com
Chez Leon: www.chezleon.com
Cicero's: www.ciceros-stl.com/
The Crossing: http//web.mac.com/thecrossing/LILUMA_AND_
CROSSING_HOMEPAGE/Front_Page.html
Cunetto House of Pasta: www.cunetto.com/
Cyrano's: www.saucemagazine.com/cyranos/
Dewey's: www.deweyspizza.com/stlouis
Dominic's: www.dominicsrestaurant.com/
Dubliner: www.dublinerstl.com/
Duff's: www.dineatduffs.com
Eleven Eleven Mississippi: www.1111-m.com/
Farotto's: www.farottos.com
Faust's: www.adamsmark.com
Feraro's Jersey Style Pizza: www.jerseystylepizza.com/
Fitz's: www.fitzsrootbeer.com/
Flannery's Pub: www.flanneryspub.com/Pub/
Fleming's Prime Steakhouse: www.flemingssteakhouse.com/
Fortel's Pizza Den: www.fortelspizzaden.com/
Goody Goody Diner: www.goodygoodydiner.com/
Giovanni's on the Hill: www.giovannisonthehill.com/
I Fratellini: www.saucemagazine.com/ifratellini/
Il Bel Lago: www.ilbellagosaintlouis.com/
Imo's Pizza: www.imospizza.com/

Iron Barley: www.ironbarley.com/
J. F. Sanfilippo's: www.jfsanfilippos.com/
j j twig's: www.jjtwigsstl.com/
Joe Boccardi's: www.joeboccardis.com/
John Mineo's Italian Restaurant: www.johnmineos.com/
Kaldi's: www.kaldiscoffee.com/page.aspx?article=locations
Kemoll's: www.kemolls.com/
Lombardo's Restaurants: www.lombardosrestaurants.com/
Lucas Park Grille: www.lucasparkgrille.com
McMurphy's: www.stpatrickcenter.org/McMurphysGrill.aspx
Moxy: www.moxybistro.com
Niche: www.nichestlouis.com/
O.T. Hodge Chile Parlor: www.othodge.com/
Ozzie's: www.ozziesrestaurantandsportsbar.com/
Paul Mineo's Trattoria: http://paulmineos.com/
Pasta House Company: www.pastahouse.com
Pepper Stone Steak House: http://pepperstonesteakhouse.com/
Pho Grand: www.phogrand.com
Racanelli's: www.racanellis.com/
Remy's Kitchen and Wine Bar: www.allgreatrestaurants.com/page.
asp?id=8&name=Remys
Revival: http://revivalstl.com/index.php?option=com_
frontpage&Itemid=1
Rich and Charlie's: www.richandcharlies.com/
Ruth's Chris Steak House: www.ruthschris.com/
St. Louis Originals: www.stlouisoriginals.com
Sauce Magazine: www.saucemagazine.com
Savor: www.saucemagazine.com/savor/
Spiro's Chesterfield and St. Charles: www.spiros-restaurant.com/
SqWires: www.sqwires.com/
Sub Zero Vodka Bar: http://subzerovodkabar.com/frm.subzero.008.php
Surf & Sirloin: www.surfandsirloin.com/Menu/Directions.aspx
Tenderloin Room: www.tenderloinroom.com/
Tony's: www.saucemagazine.com/tonys/
Top of the Riverfront: www.millenniumhotels.com/millenniumstlouis/
restaurant/index.html
Trailhead Brewing: www.trailheadbrewing.com/
Truffles: www.trufflesinladue.com/
Vin de Set: www.1111-m.com/vindeset/index.htm
Vito's: www.vitosstl.com/

Restaurant Guides
Joe and Ann Lemons Pollack: www.stlouiseats.typepad.com/
Riverfront Times Restaurant Guide: http://restaurants.riverfronttimes.
com/search/restaurants.php
Sauce Magazine Restaurant Guide: www.saucemagazine.com/restguide.php

Trade Organizations
Missouri Restaurant Association: www.morestaurants.org/
National Restaurant Association: www.restaurant.org/

Books
Dining In – St. Louis by J.A. Baer and Cecile K. Lowenhaupt (Peanut Butter Publishing, 1979).
The Days & Nights of the Central West End (Second Edition), edited by Jeff Fister (Virginia Publishing Company, 2007).

Chapter 2: Food Manufacturers

Websites
Batter Up! Cookies: www.batterupcookies.com/
Berhanu Organic: www.berhanuorganic.com/
Bissingers Chocolate Experience: www.experiencebissingers.com/index.html
Bissinger's Handcrafted Chocolates: www.bissingers.com/
Black Bear Bakery: http://blackbearbakery.org/
Breadsmith of St. Louis: www.breadsmith.com/locations/stlouis.html
The Brownie Factory: www.browniefactory.com/
Carla's St. Louis Vinegar Sauce: http://carlaskitchenllc.com/index.htm
Chocolate Chocolate Chocolate: www.chocolatechocolate.com/index.htm
Companion: www.companionstl.com/home.html
Cravings Gourmet Desserts: www.cravingsonline.com/sys-tmpl/door/
The Cupcakery: www.thecupcakery.net/
Dad's Cookie Company: www.dadscookies.com/
The Daily Bread: www.thedbcafe.com/
DB Gourmet Cookies: www.dbgourmetcookies.com/
Dogtown Pizza: www.dogtownpizza.com/home.html
Fazio's Bakery: www.faziosbakery.com/
Fitz's Root Beer: www.fitzsrootbeer.com/
Florence's HomeStyle Cha-Cha: www.florenceshomestyle.com/index.html
Gelato di Riso: www.gelatodiriso.com/
Gibbons Bee Farm: www.gibbonsbeefarm.com/
Great Harvest Bread Company: www.greatharvest.com/
Gus' Pretzels: www.guspretzels.com/
Hanks' Cheesecakes: www.hankscheesecakes.com
Happy Dogs Hot Sauce: www.happydogshotsauce.com/
Hautly Cheese Company: www.hautly.com/
Jilly's Cupcake Bar: www.jillyscupcakebar.com/Home.html
Kakao Chocolates: www.kakaochocolate.com/Store/default.aspx
Kaldi's Coffee Roasting Company: www.kaldiscoffee.com/
Lake Forest Confections: www.lakeforestconfections.com/
Lasco Foods: www.lascofoods.com
Little Pleasures Soups and Dips: www.lifes-little-pleasures.com/
Louis Maull Company: http://maull.com/
Manzo Importing Company: www.manzoskitchen.com/Home.html
Missouri Mercantile: www.missourimercantile.com/
Moon Day Soul Treats: www.moondaysoul.com/index.html
Mound City Shelled Nut Company: www.moundcity.com/index.htm
My House Salt: www.myhousesalt.com/
Panera Bread Company: www.panerabread.com/
Pratzel's Bakery: www.pratzels.com/
Randy's Famous Salsa: http://randysfamoussalsa.com/
Rosciglione Bakery: http://rosciglione.tripod.com/
Ronnoco Coffee: www.ronnoco.com/
Serendipity Homemade Ice Cream: www.serendipity-icecream.com/
Super Smokers: www.supersmokers.com/
Sweeties to Go: www.sweetiestogo.com/
Switzer's Licorice: www.switzercandy.com/
Ted Drewes: www.teddrewes.com/Drewes.asp
Volpi Foods: www.volpifoods.com/VolpiFoods.htm

Books
Zion in the Valley: The Jewish Community of St. Louis, Volume 1, by Walter Ehrlich (University of Missouri Press, 1997).
Food in Missouri, by Madeline Matson (University of Missouri Press, 1994).
Immigrants on the Hill, by Garry Ross Mormino (University of Missouri Press, 2002).

Chapter 3: Groceries

Websites
Dierbergs: www.dierbergs.com
Local Harvest Grocery: www.localharvestgrocery.com/
Sappington Farmer's Market: www.sappingtonfarmersmkt.com/
Save-a-Lot Stores: www.save-a-lot.com
Schnucks Markets: www.schnucks.com
Shop 'n Save: www.shopnsave.com/sns-webapp/index.jsp
Straub's Markets: www.straubs.com
SUPERVALU Inc.: www.supervalu.com

Books
Milk Eggs Vodka: Grocery Lists Lost and Found, by Bill Keaggy (HOW Books, 2007).

Trade Organizations
Food Marketing Institute: www.fmi.org
Missouri Grocers Association: www.missourigrocers.com/
Women Grocers of America: www.nationalgrocers.org/WGA/WGA.html

Chapter 4: Farms and Farmers' Markets

Farm Websites
Bellews Creek Farm: www.localharvest.org/farms/M228
Biver Farms: www.localharvest.org/farms/M3563
Centennial Farms: www.centennialfarms.biz/inseason.html
Claverach Farm: www.claverach.com/
Eckert's Farms: www.eckerts.com/
Farrar Out Farm: www.localharvest.org/farms/M16207
Hinkebein Hills Farm: www.hinkebeinhillsfarm.com/
Kimker Hill Farm: www.localharvest.org/farms/M17777
New Roots Urban Farm: www.newrootsurbanfarm.org/
Norris Farms: www.localharvest.org/farms/M15861

Sunflower Savannah Farm: www.sunflowersavannah.com/home.html
Thies Farm: www.thiesfasm.com
Three Rivers Community Farm: /www.threeriverscommunityfarm.com/html/join_us.html
Voss Pecans: www.vosspecans.com/

Farmers' Market Websites
Clayton Farmer's Market: www.claytonfarmersmarket.com/
Ferguson Farmers' Market: www.fergusonfarmersmarket.com
Kirkwood Farmers' Market: www.kirkwoodjunction.com/default.aspx?tabid=431
Land of Goshen Community Market: www.goshenmarket.org/
Maplewood Farmers' Market: www.schlafly.com/market.shtml
St, Jacobs Farmers' Market: www.stjacobs.com/html/shopping-farmersmarkets.html
Soulard Market: www.soulardmarket.com/
Tower Grove Farmers' Market: www.tgmarket.org/

Restaurants
Five and Newstead Tower Pub: http://newsteadtowerpub.com/
Riddle's Penultimate: www.riddlescafe.com/

Books
Animal, Vegetable, Miracle: A Year of Food Life, by Barbara Kingsolver, Camille Kingsolver, and Steven L. Hopp (HarperCollins, 2007).
In Defense of Food: An Eater's Manifesto, by Michael Pollan (Penguin Books, 2008).

Organizations
AgriMissouri: www.agrimissouri.com/farmersmarket.htm
EatHereStL (Andy Ayers): www.EatHereStL.com
Kitchen Gardeners International: www.kitchengardeners.org
Local Harvest, Inc.: www.localharvest.org/organic-farms/
Missouri Farmers' Market Blog: http://mofarmersmarket.blogspot.com/
Slow Food USA: www.slowfoodusa.org/
USDA Statistics: www.nass.usda.gov/census/census02/volume1/mo/index2.htm.)

Chapter 5: Breweries, Wineries, and Watering Holes
Brewery Websites
Anheuser-Busch Cos.: www.anheuser-busch.com
Augusta Brewing Company: www.augustabrewing.com
Brewers Association: www.beertown.org/ba/index.html
Griesedieck Brothers Brewing Corporation: www.gb-beer.com
Illinois breweries: www.americanbreweriana.org/history/bvil.htm
Morgan Street Brewery: www.morganstreetbrewery.com
O'Fallon Brewery: www.ofallonbrewery.com
St. Louis Brewery: www.schlafly.com
Square One Brewery: www.squareonebrewery.com/index.htm
Trailhead Brewing Company: www.trailheadbrewingcompany.com

Brewery Books
Making Friends Is Our Business: 100 Years of Anheuser-Busch, by Roland Krebs (The Cuneo Press, 1953).
Ambitious Brew: The Story of American Beer, by Maureen Ogle (Harcourt Inc. 2006).
A History of Anheuser-Busch, 1852-1933, by Ronald Jan Plavchan (Ayer Company, 1975).
A New Religion in Mecca: Memoir of a Renegade Brewery in St. Louis, by Tom Schlafly (Virginia Publishing Company, 2006).

Winery Websites
Augusta Winery: www.augustawinery.com
Illinois Grape Growers and Vintners Association: www.illinoiswine.com/
Institute for Continental Climate Viticulture and Enology: http://iccve.missouri.edu/about/
Mary Michelle Winery & Vineyard: www.illinois-wine.com
Missouri Department of Agriculture: www.mda.mo.gov/Market/wineries.htm
Missouri Wine & Grape Board: www.missouriwine.org/wineries/default.htm
Missouri Wine Experience: www.missouriwinecountry.com
Montelle Winery: www.montelle.com/index.asp.
33 Wine Shop and Tasting Bar: www.33wine.com

Winery Books
Exploring Missouri Wine Country, by Brett Dufur (Pebble Publishing, 2007).

Watering Hole Websites
Allen Ginsberg Trust: www.allenginsberg.org
Blueberry Hill: www.blueberryhill.com
Gaslight Square: www.gaslightsquare.org
John Goodman: www.imdb.com/name/nm0000422/maindetails
O'Leary's: www.olearys2.admitonevip.com

Watering Hole Books
Harry's St. Louis Guide to Taverns, Pubs, Saloons and Other Drinking Establishments, by Dan Brennan and Steve Weaver (Knight Publishing Company. 1980) .
The Days & Nights of the Central West End (Second Edition), edited by Jeff Fister (Virginia Publishing Company, 2007) .
Taverns & Travelers, by Paton Yoder (Indiana University Press, 1969).